INTRODUCTION TO THE CRITICAL STUDY OF THE TEXT OF THE HEBREW BIBLE

J. WEINGREEN

Emeritus Fellow of Trinity College, Dublin
Emeritus Professor of Hebrew
University of Dublin

CLARENDON PRESS · OXFORD
OXFORD UNIVERSITY PRESS · NEW YORK
1982

Oxford University Press, Walton Street, Oxford OX2 6DP
London Glasgow New York Toronto
Delhi Bombay Calcutta Madras Karachi
Kuala Lumpur Singapore Hong Kong Tokyo
Nairobi Dar es Salaam Cape Town
Melbourne Auckland
and associate companies in
Beirut Berlin Ibadan Mexico City

British Library Cataloguing in Publication Data
Weingreen, Jacob
Introduction to the critical study of the text
of the Hebrew Bible.
1. Bible: Hebrew—Criticism, Textual
I. Title
220'.44   BS471   80-40867
ISBN 0-19-815453-4

Set by Typeset International Ltd., Jerusalem
Printed in the United States of America

Printing (last digit): 9 8 7 6 5 4 3 2 1

CONTENTS

ABBREVIATIONS

AV – Authorized Version of the Bible

JB – Jerusalem Bible

RSV – Revised Standard Version of the Bible

LXX – Septuagint: ancient Greek Version of the Bible

Targum J – Aramaic Version of the Bible relating to the prophets and attributed to one Jonathan

1QIs^a – Qumran scroll of Isaiah

INTRODUCTION

This book is directed primarily to students of the Hebrew Bible. Its aim is to present an acceptable scheme and a practical apparatus for the critical study of the text of the Hebrew Bible. In this presentation an important feature will be the phenomenon of human fallibility which manifested itself in the professional copying of ancient manuscripts. Scattered throughout the writings of the Hebrew Bible are instances of miscopying due to a variety of reasons but ultimately to be attributed to human fallibility or misunderstanding. Information of special relevance to our study will be derived from references in the Talmud to the recognition by the Rabbis of that period of textual difficulties arising from types of copyists' errors. An analysis of directed rabbinic corrections of faulty texts leads to the postulation of guide-lines in, firstly, recognizing copyists' errors and, secondly, the way in which such problems may be resolved. It should, perhaps, be mentioned at the outset that the scope of textual criticism is not limited to the detection of errors which had become perpetuated in the authorized Hebrew text, though the main burden of this book will be concerned with this problem. It should be said, furthermore, that though the phenomenon of scribal error may appear to loom large in any presentation of textual criticism, the incidence of such corruptions is comparatively very small indeed. In fact, the presence of comparatively so few errors in the text of the Hebrew Bible testifies to the general faithful copying of biblical manuscripts.

Our first task is to provide a concise but adequate description of the discipline known as textual criticism. This is the subject matter of Chapter 1. In this chapter mention will be made of some of the objections to textual criticism expressed by conservative students of the Bible and by ill-informed critics of this discipline. Though the textual critic is not called upon to allay their fears, their objections should not be ignored but should be dealt with sensibly. It might be somewhat reassuring to them if it is pointed out that some of the guide-lines which today govern the critical study of the text of the Hebrew Bible are not of recent scholarly origin but, in their essentials, may be traced back to early rabbinic sources in the Talmud. This judgement is made from a study of rabbinic admonitions directed to professional copyists of the Hebrew Scriptures and from a categorization of their lists of scribal errors in the Hebrew text, as indicated by the corrections supplied by them, to which the attention of the reader is drawn.

Though it is in no way suggested that the main principles of modern textual criticism were enunciated by the talmudic Rabbis, it may be said that some of these are implicit in their official textual notes on the Hebrew Bible. Broadly speaking one may conclude that some of the main guide-lines of textual criticism were, however indirectly, anticipated by them. To validate this proposition Chapter 2 is concerned with what we have termed 'Rabbinic Antecedents of Textual Criticism'. The student may be agreeably surprised to learn that axioms recorded in the Talmud relating to the serious study of the Hebrew Bible represent a sensible approach, expressing basic postulates which are highly acceptable to the textual critic today.

Chapter 3 is devoted to the scope and the limitations of textual criticism. Because the range of its interest goes beyond the identification and correction of copyists' errors, it is necessary to indicate both its wider interests and its proper confines. Being one of several avenues of biblical study, textual criticism must, where relevant, take note of literary criticism, literary documents outside the Hebrew Bible, and the advances made in Semitic philology.

Chapter 4 cites specific and typical examples of rabbinic corrections of faulty Hebrew texts. An analysis of these point to what may be described as recurring types of scribal error.

Introduction

The rabbinic list of textual errors and their directed corrections is by no means complete, as is evidenced from the many instances of faulty texts which were not noted by them, to some of which we shall refer. The general pattern of examination adopted in this chapter in dealing with textual corruption, where possible, is as follows. We shall firstly cite a particular type of error noted and corrected by the Rabbis. This will be followed by an instance of the same type of error not noted (and so not corrected) by them, but identifiable by observation and often by external aids, such as duplicated passages in the Hebrew Bible and the evidence of the ancient versions. We shall then proceed to offer the appropriate correction of the faulty element in the text.

Chapter 5 is devoted to samples of textual errors which cannot be placed under any category of recurring scribal error. In such cases the judgement of the scholar will be brought to bear on the elucidation of the textual difficulty. If the only avenue open to him is by way of conjecture, the context will be taken into account. That is to say, the emendation offered will not be an arbitrary suggestion, but will be the result of serious and careful consideration. It is sometimes found that a textual difficulty due to an enigmatic word or phrase may be solved by reference to that word or phrase in another Semitic language, where the true meaning has survived but had been lost in Hebrew. Such a solution, in restoring a lost meaning, is not a textual emendation and, strictly speaking, is outside the scope of textual criticism.

Chapter 6 is devoted to an examination of glosses and editorial notes. These are, as will be shown, items of extra material which were incorporated into the text of the Hebrew Bible and thus were not part of the original composition. Because glosses and editorial notes are informative, they are indicative of attitudes in the exposition of sacred texts during the formative years of the Hebrew Bible and thus constitute an important element in the very early exposition of sacred texts and are, on that account, in themselves worthy of study as a small corpus of literature. In this chapter these phenomena are identified and their significance explained.

What may not be sufficiently realized is that the textual critic, equipped with his accumulated knowledge of Hebrew and other Semitic languages, is nevertheless following, in part, the pattern revealed by the study of the rabbinic treatment of difficult or erroneous texts of the Hebrew Bible. In presenting what may be described as a line of continuity, in this respect, from the talmudic Rabbis to the modern textual critics, our aim is not simply to provide some assurance to the conservative sceptic, but to reveal an important early element in the history of Hebrew biblical studies which is of significance in its own right.

Since this book is designed specifically for the student of Hebrew biblical texts and its aim is to present an introduction to, and not a comprehensive review of, textual criticism, its size has been advisedly restricted. In the initial stages of the student's introduction to this discipline too much information could lead to confusion. It is hoped that, once the student has grasped the principles underlying textual criticism with understanding, he will be able intelligently to follow a standard critical commentary on the Hebrew text he is studying. It seems sensible, from his point of view, to leave the account of the meticulous work of the Massoretes and of the families of Hebrew biblical manuscripts to a later time, when he will be in a position to understand them and appreciate their significance. From the same consideration, detailed information about the main ancient versions of the Hebrew Bible has not been given, though an outline of these and their place in the scheme of textual criticism is necessary. A final consideration in keeping the size of this book to a minimum is that, in these days of the ever-increasing cost of books, a small book is more likely to be within the student's financial capacity.

It is assumed that the student reading this book will have some knowledge of the Hebrew language and that he will have

Introduction

his Hebrew Bible before him. Therefore the references to chapters and verses are those of the Hebrew Bible, since the enumeration of certain Psalms in the ancient Greek (Septuagint) and in some English versions does not correspond with that of the Hebrew Bible. In the book of Jeremiah in particular the arrangement of some of the chapters in the ancient Greek version is quite different from that in the Hebrew Bible. Where, however, reference is made to texts in the Septuagint or English versions which are arranged differently from what we find in the Hebrew Bible, a note to this effect will, of course, be given, so that the student will find the corresponding reference.

I have been rather sparing in the provision of footnotes. Since this book is directed to students and not to mature scholars, copious footnotes could have the effect of distracting the student's attention from the main theme of the paragraph, particularly where continuity in presentation is essential. In the early stages of study, supplementary material is not always helpful nor will an account of scholarly disagreements necessarily be enlightening. The art of presenting a new discipline is in knowing not only what should be dealt with but also what should be excluded and left to a later stage in the student's studies.

Trinity College
University of Dublin   J. WEINGREEN

1

THE NATURE OF TEXTUAL CRITICISM

In the modern study of the Hebrew Bible there are several lines of approach which all converge into a coherent pattern of the study of the culture and history of ancient Israel. These are mainly linguistic, literary, historical, and archaeological—all within the background of ancient Near Eastern history and civilization. Our interest in this book is centred upon the text of the Hebrew Bible though, occasionally, we shall have to refer to some of the other related disciplines. In order the better to understand the special role of the textual critic, it will be found profitable first to mention briefly the function of his counterpart, the literary critic. By contrast, the aim of the textual critic will become clearer.

Broadly speaking, the literary critic is concerned with the problem of identifying, and thus establishing, the authorship and date of a given literary composition, whether or not the text in question bears an autograph. He will describe the style of the composition as being either characteristic of the author or in line with a known pattern. He will also seek out the motivation of the author or, it may be, of the editor. If the biblical literary critic subscribes to the so-called Documentary Hypothesis, he will endeavour to disentangle the different literary strands which, it is claimed by this School, together constitute the Pentateuch (or Hexateuch, if the book of Joshua is to be included with the Pentateuch in the one corpus of literature). On the other hand, the textual critic is primarily concerned with the actual wording of the text of the Hebrew Bible, as it has come down to us in the authorized Jewish recension known as the massoretic (see p. 11). It will readily be understood that these two areas of study often complement each other. Since the prime essential for the literary critic, as for the textual critic, is correct texts as intended by their authors he will take cognizance of restorations offered by the textual critic in texts where corruption had set in through faulty copying or by alterations in the wording of the text made in a later generation because of religious scruple generated by post-biblical thought. On the other hand, the textual critic may sometimes find that what the literary critic has to say about a certain biblical composition could influence his understanding of the text and help him repair any distortion which may have set in. Though their respective studies are concerned with the same Hebrew Bible and sometimes with the same texts, their special interests should, nevertheless, be clearly demarcated.

We now proceed to enunciate some of the basic postulates which mark the first steps in the critical study of any ancient literary document, quite irrespective of whether or not it is free from linguistic or textual difficulties. The first assumption is, surely, that the author of a given literary document wrote in a language which was native to, or at least understood by, the people to whom his writing was addressed. One must, furthermore, postulate that the author designed his writing in a literary form intended to be intelligible to his readers. In the following chapter we shall point to the remarkable fact that these two basic postulates are inherent in official pronouncements made by the talmudic Rabbis in their approach to the objective study of the Hebrew Bible.

It is taken for granted, of course, that the textual critic is highly competent in the language of the literary composition under his critical scrutiny. He will adopt the cautionary attitude, in the first place, of making sure that the problem encountered is in the Hebrew text before him and that the difficulty is not to be attributed to any inadequacy in our present knowledge of the language or of unsuspected meanings of Hebrew phrasings. If, then, after careful study, it becomes evident beyond reasonable doubt that somehow corruption had been introduced into the text, the procedure appropriate to the task will be somewhat as follows. Firstly, if possible, the element of corruption must be identified and, once this is recognized, it often becomes clear to the critic how the corruption came to be introduced into the text. It will be found generally that miscopyings which are accidental may be accounted for in terms of human fallibility, through misreadings of words and phrases or misunderstandings of the intent of the author. By identifying the error and explaining how it came about, the textual critic may then be able to remove the disruptive element and restore the text to its original form as written by the author or as it left the hands of the final editor. In Chapter 4 we shall deal with such cases in the manner described here.

There are situations, however, where the identification of a corruption in a text may be well founded but the explanation of its intrusion may elude the scholar. In such a dilemma the textual critic will have two possible options available to him. He may, on the one hand, simply concede that the solution to the problem before him is at present beyond his ability. On the other hand, he may offer a conjectural emendation which is by no means arbitrary, but will be based upon his understanding of the context of the whole passage, taking into account the letters of the word or phrase under scrutiny. In the latter instance, however, there will be the reservation that his proposed reconstruction is tentative and that it is the best he can produce in the circumstances. He will readily admit the feasibility of his conjectural reconstruction being invalidated and the correct solution achieved either through the new knowledge of a later age or by another, more perceptive, scholar. A spirit of moderation now pervades the work of the textual critic, even when speculation is the only course open to him. This attitude is in sharp contrast to the one which permeated textual criticism in biblical studies in the latter part of the nineteenth and in the early years of the twentieth centuries, during which period a bewildering proliferation of proposed emendations of biblical texts developed. The student was often required to take note of a variety of competing emendations of a word or phrase in a biblical Hebrew text and he was left more perplexed through this exercise than by the presence of the textual difficulty.

It is beyond the scope of this book, and so irrelevant, to introduce and deal with questions which properly lie within the province of religious debate, such as the personal affirmation or denial of the inspirational character of the Hebrew Scriptures in terms of direct divine revelation. However, whatever the attitude of the student of the Hebrew Bible may be, it may be useful to make a general observation which is applicable equally to those who affirm and to those who deny that the authors of the various books of the Hebrew Bible wrote under divine inspiration. That is, that the transmission of the sacred texts was achieved by human hands in the continuous copying of these texts over many generations by professional copyists for use in the liturgy and for teaching and study. In fact, Tora scrolls used in the synagogue liturgy are, even today, copied by hand by expert copyists who are called Sopherim 'scribes'.[1] How far back this process goes is difficult to determine, but it can be demonstrated that evidence is forthcoming of the making of copies of the sacred texts during the formative years of the various sections of the Hebrew Bible.

It might sound rather trite to observe that even professionally experienced people are prone to fallibility in their specialized work, in spite of the scrupulous care taken by them in the execution of their tasks. Yet, it is important to point to this phenomenon of human fallibility in the copying of manuscripts, for it is one of the main justifications for the construction and application of an apparatus of textual criticism to deal with textual corruption. In the following chapters we shall provide ample illustrations of erroneous copying made by copyists and perpetuated in the text of the Hebrew

---

[1] The profession of the hand copyist continued in the offices of solicitors till the invention of the typewriter. Leases on houses bought were copied by hand by a clerk known as an amanuensis and his work was not always free from error.

Bible by subsequent copyists. The talmudic Rabbis were vividly aware of the kinds of corruptions likely to be accidentally introduced into texts being prepared by copyists of their time, as is evidenced by the cautionary advice and the directives they gave to professional copyists (pp. 19–22). Their official corrections of faulty Hebrew texts point to the same conclusion (see Chapter 4).

In this connection it will be of some interest to mention an incident which occurred recently in a synagogue one Sabbath morning during the recital of the weekly portion of the Tora by the cantor. As the congregation was following the reading of a passage, the cantor suddenly stopped his reading and a hushed silence fell upon the worshippers. It was immediately realized by them that, in the modern scroll of the Tora on the cantor's desk an error which had hitherto eluded detection had been discovered. In accordance with rabbinic practice the Tora scroll was immediately closed and solemnly and silently returned to the ark. Another scroll was taken from the ark and brought to the cantor's reading desk, where it was unrolled till the section which was being read was reached. The cantor then continued his reading from the second scroll precisely from the point at which he had stopped in the first scroll. No doubt the synagogue authorities complied with the rabbinic rule laid down in the Babylonian Talmud Ketubot 19b that not more than thirty days were to elapse between the discovery of an error in a Tora scroll and its correction. This incident is mentioned here to drive home the point that, even in our time, the introduction of errors in the professional copying of a Tora scroll can occur. The rabbinic exhortation to copyists of the Hebrew biblical text to be vigiliant against accidental miscopying is still valid today.

From the samples of faulty texts in the Hebrew Bible which are provided in Chapter 4 it will become apparent that ancient copyists were prone to make the kind of errors in transcription which anyone would be likely to make today in the copying of a text, whether by hand or on a typewriter. In a literary composition printed for publication it is not unusual that an author, in checking the proof sheets, may come across errors made by the compositor, in spite of the professional skill, experience, and scrupulous care which this specialist brought to his work. When the student realizes that human fallibility explains the intrusion of errors into the copying of texts not only in antiquity but even in our own time, he will understand that the function of the textual critic of the Hebrew Bible is to try to repair any damage done to the text through accidental faulty copying and thus to restore it to its correct form, as it left the hands of the author or editor.

At this juncture it should be pointed out that the range of textual criticism is not restricted to the identification and elimination of errors in the Hebrew Bible. Variant traditional readings account for a considerable number of discrepant readings found in duplicated texts in the Hebrew Bible itself, as well as in the renderings of the ancient versions and in readings of the Qumran biblical texts[2] as compared with those in the massoretic Hebrew Bible. Often such variants may each have a claim to validity as much as the ones adopted in the massoretic Hebrew Bible. In such instances one might simply note these discrepancies without indulging in any subjective preference for one or the other.

We must, however, make reference to another phenomenon in some Hebrew biblical texts, that is to deliberate alterations

---

[2] These manuscripts were found in 1947 and subsequent years at Qumran in the Judean desert near the Dead Sea and are consequently also known as the Dead Sea Scrolls. Of the biblical manuscripts found, all the books of the Hebrew Bible are represented, with the exception of the book of Esther. One copy of Isaiah is complete and another has survived only in part. The book of the prophet Habakkuk is accompanied by a commentary which relates the prophet's utterances to the situation of the Qumran sect. Curiously, the third chapter, which is a Psalm, is absent in this manuscript, though there are several unused lines on the last section. This fact indicates that this isolated Psalm had not yet been attached to this small book. There are also a number of non-biblical compositions, but our interest will be in the biblical manuscripts, though most of these are fragmentary. Because these biblical manuscripts were in use during the first century BC to the first century CE, they antedate all existing medieval manuscripts of the Hebrew Bible by over 1,000 years.

made by the Rabbis in perfectly correct texts—and a number of such changes have been faithfully recorded by them—with the aim of purging expressions regarded by them as indelicate or liable to be construed by the reader as blasphemous when taken in their literal sense. The Rabbis achieved their purpose by directing the substitution of different but inoffensive words for those in the text. In some instances the words in the written text were actually changed: in other instances no change in the written text was made, but the substitution was to be made orally. In unpointed consonantal texts, such as the Tora scrolls used in synagogue services, the literate and experienced reader is expected to know of, and thus to make, the directed substitutions in the readings. In the printed Hebrew Bibles the attention of the reader is drawn to the directed substitutions by the retention of the consonantal words in the text but with the attachment of the vowel-points of the word to be read, which thus produces hybrid, impossible words. These textual irregularities are illustrated in Chapter 3, pp. 26—29.

Turning now to faulty readings in the massoretic Hebrew Bible to which the talmudic Rabbis drew attention we observe that each noted error is accompanied by a directive that the correction which they supplied is to be made by the reader orally. That is to say, the erroneous word or expression was not to be corrected in the written text but, in spite of its being identified as an error, it was to be retained without any alteration whatsoever. Such a procedure might be pronounced by pedantic scholars as unscientific and unfortunate, since it resulted in the perpetuation of recognized errors in the text. Yet, if we look at such situations from the rabbinic point of view, we shall appreciate that, even though the motives of the Rabbis may have been essentially religious, they were not devoid of good sense. By this unscientific procedure they achieved a dual aim which may be regarded as eminently reasonable. On the one hand they ensured that the reader of the sacred text would make the correct reading while, on the other hand, they preserved the text from any possible future alteration. In fact, when we look at the work of the modern textual critic, we find that his procedure is parallel to that of the Rabbis described above. His critical observations and his proposed textual restorations of correct, original readings are external to the massoretic Hebrew Bible. These are offered in published studies, commentaries, and translations of the Hebrew text, while the identifiable errors are retained in the text without any alterations whatsoever. Following the pattern of the printed Hebrew Bibles where massoretic textual notes are placed at the bottom of the pages as footnotes, Kittel's critical edition of the Hebrew Bible likewise places approved critical notes at the foot of the pages. There were, indeed, some scholars at the end of the nineteenth century who published, what they claimed to be corrected Hebrew editions of Isaiah and the Psalms which, in many instances, differed radically from the massoretic Hebrew texts. Such procedures are no longer indulged in by textual critics today. We are aware that many of the proposed emendations may be tentative and, because textual critics are not always in agreement in the restorations offered, it is not possible, even if it were desirable, to produce an agreed and fully corrected edition of the Hebrew Bible.

One further observation relevant to textual criticism should be made. When the compositions of the Hebrew Bible were written, biblical Hebrew was a living, spoken language. As such it possessed a range in vocabulary and grammatical constructions much wider than what we have gleaned from the literature preserved in the Hebrew Bible. In recent times Hebrew words and grammatical formulations whose meanings had been lost have been recovered through the comparative study of Semitic languages, of which Hebrew is a member. Many words and phrases which formerly were unintelligible and consequently condemned as faulty have proved subsequently to have been in normal usage current in biblical Hebrew. Their meanings had been lost either because of their isolated occurrence in the Hebrew Bible or, alternatively, because of their close resemblance to, and so their mistaken identification with, familiar Hebrew words. By reference to such words or phrases in another sister Semitic language where their meanings *are* known, their recovery for biblical Hebrew is often made possible (pp. 91–92). When the scholar comes across a word or a phrase which, at first glance, appears to be enigmatic, he will not condemn it out of hand as being an error in transcription, but will turn to other Semitic languages to ascertain whether or not its true meaning may be achieved by reference to a parallel word or phrase in one of the other languages. If this kind of exercise is successful and alteration in the word is found to be unnecessary, then we consider this procedure to be outside the scope of textual criticism, for it properly belongs to the province of Semitic philology.

One final consideration, not as yet sufficiently studied but which could have an indirect influence on the true understanding of simple words or phrases which, when taken literally, seem to be out of keeping with the general context of the verse, is the following. When biblical Hebrew was a living, spoken language, it manifested characteristics which are inherent in any spoken language. One of these is that a speaker (or writer) may use a simple expression in a particular context, but his intent is not to convey its literal sense but, rather, some implication indicated by the context. An example from contemporary English will illustrate this phenomenon well. When two people are talking about a third person and one of them says to the other 'I will talk to him', there are three possible implications conveyed by this expression, as indicated by the theme of their conversation. It could mean (*a*) 'I will find out from him what he wants or what he said', (*b*) 'I will reprimand him', or (*c*) 'I will intercede with him on your behalf'. What is of significance is that, because the speaker (or writer) and the listener (or reader) speak the same language, the implied active sense is immediately understood by the person addressed. In texts where the implications of simple words or phrases in their contexts are not recognized and a direct understanding of the word produces ambiguity, resort is often made to interpretations of what the writer meant to convey or to some emendation designed to produce good sense. These may be as many and as varied as the number of commentators or textual critics. An understanding of this feature of speech (which is reflected in writing) often solves a textual difficulty and renders the need for interpretation, and certainly for textual emendation, quite unnecessary.

2
RABBINIC ANTECEDENTS OF
TEXTUAL CRITICISM

WHAT might be termed 'rabbinic antecedents' of modern textual criticism are well attested in rabbinic literature, both talmudic and post-talmudic. In this chapter we shall demonstrate that there was a serious rabbinic approach to the study of the Hebrew Bible, in spite of the practice of expounding biblical texts for purely homiletical purposes which, within its own sphere, was regarded as legitimate. The two processes operated side by side but were, nevertheless, meant to be quite distinct.

We have at our disposal a collection of official rabbinic critical and informational notes on the Hebrew text of the Bible and this is known as the מָסֹרֶת Massōreth. This Hebrew noun is derived from the verb מָסַר (*māsar*) meaning 'handed over', 'delivered' (of which the Latin equivalent is *trado*, from which the English word *tradition* comes). *Massoreth*, then, means 'that which has been handed on' from one generation to another and so 'tradition'. This collection of textual notes is attributed to the rabbinic authorities of Tiberias in the seventh and eighth centuries CE who are designated as בַּעֲלֵי הַמָּסֹרֶת 'the keepers of the tradition'. From this Hebrew word *Massoreth* the term *Massoretes* was coined to denote the Tiberian textual authorities and the adjective *massoretic* to indicate the traditional, authorized recension of the Hebrew Bible which has come down to us.

The Massoretes were not innovators in the literary activity of providing critical and informational notes on the text of the Hebrew Bible. Their contribution represents the orderly arrangement of details in, and the culmination of, a literary process which was in operation centuries earlier. This rabbinic preoccupation with the text of the Hebrew Bible may be traced back, stage by stage, at least to the late post-exile period of the history of Israel. We have, in the first place, the records in the Talmud which indicate an established tradition, presupposing a history which culminated in these talmudic records. Then we have evidence of this kind of literary activity during the formative years of the Hebrew Bible which we can even trace back to the period antedating the Greek version, the Septuagint (usually designated as the *LXX*) that is, before the third to second centuries BC. The antiquity of this literary process becomes evident from the presence in the texts of both the Hebrew Bible and of the Septuagint of incorporated textual notes, as we shall explain in Chapter 6 (p. 86). .

Comparisons between readings in certain Hebrew massoretic texts and those in the *LXX* version of the same texts (of the third to second centuries BC) on the one hand, and of these texts in the Qumran (Dead Sea) scrolls, particularly the complete scroll of Isaiah (in use during the first centuries BC and CE) on the other hand, reveal the following fact. Manuscripts of the Hebrew Bible which were in use (for liturgical purposes and for study) before the fixing of a standard text (believed to have been attempted about 135 CE), when compared with each other, occasionally exhibited discrepancies in the readings of words and phrases in the same texts. There are instances in the Talmud of a biblical quotation differing from the massoretic text. In the tractate Sabbath 56a the end of the verse in 2 Samuel 16: 4 is quoted as אֶמְצָא חֵן בְּעֵינֵי הַמֶּלֶךְ 'Let me find favour in the eyes of the king', whereas the massoretic text reads אֶמְצָא חֵן בְּעֵינֶיךָ אֲדוֹנִי הַמֶּלֶךְ 'Let me find favour in your eyes, my lord king'. Does the talmudic variant represent a different textual tradition or is it just an oral misquotation recorded? If this were merely a misquotation, it is surprising that it was not corrected when subsequently recorded in writing. Sabbath 116a makes reference to the sacred texts of the Sadducees which were regarded as unworthy, thereby implying the possibility of variations in readings from the authorized text of the Pharisee Rabbis.

Because of the inspirational character attributed to the

Hebrew Bible by the Rabbis, it was for them the divine authority from which much of their traditional and continually expanding Judaism was derived. Their acute need was, clearly, the establishment of a text which was authorized and thus immutable. When confronted with variant readings in the same passage in biblical manuscripts in actual use, they had of necessity to resolve the dilemma of which reading was to be accepted as the official one. What mechanism could be devised to meet this perplexing situation? We have no direct evidence of any principles which they followed in determining between discrepant readings in manuscripts, but an indication of procedure could be read into a statement in the Palestinian Talmud, tractate *Ta'anit* IV. It is recorded here that three scrolls of the Tora were found in the Temple court, one having a discrepant reading compared with the readings in the other two. The reading in the two manuscripts was adopted as against the variant reading in the third one. Does this signify that they generally applied the simple criterion of accepting the reading which was in the majority of manuscripts in their care? It may be argued with some justification that such a mode of arbitrary selection is highly unscientific, in that it involved the distinct possibility of their adopting, and thereby perpetuating, faulty readings in their authorized biblical text. That this is precisely what happened is attested by the fact that they had to supply official corrections to numerous textual errors which had become established in the text. In response to the argument that the adoption of majority readings by the Rabbis not only is unproven, but is an unsatisfactory method of resolving the problem of conflicting texts, one may remind the reader that the concern of the Rabbis was of a religious nature and not necessarily scientific. On the other hand, there is the view that the fluidity in manuscript readings which was evident in early talmudic times suggests the existence of several recensions of the Hebrew Scriptures. One underlay the text translated by the *LXX,* another is indicated by the Qumran scrolls, and a third was adopted by the Rabbis and became the massoretic text.

If we view the dilemma of dealing with discrepant readings from the point of view of the Rabbis and if, in the absence of direct information, we consider as likely their applying the unscientific criterion of majority readings in manuscripts as decisive or their adoption of one recension of the Bible as the authorized one, we shall find that their reasoning was not lacking in good sense. Had they decided that authorized readings were to be determined by the objective study of discrepant readings in biblical manuscripts the uncertainties would not have been removed. A purely scholarly handling of such situations might have given rise to schools of variant readings, each one defending its own conclusions with reasoned arguments, as is the situation today among textual critics. The Rabbis would still have been faced with the responsibility of deciding which of the rival claims to original readings was valid. An analogy of this kind of unsatisfactory situation brought about by scholarly methods is provided by the Talmud in the realm of rabbinic legislation. There are many instances of conflicting rulings on legal or religious questions made by different rabbinic schools or by individual Rabbis, each validating the conclusions reached with some form of reasoning. Where such conflicting rulings cannot be harmonized or reconciled, the presiding rabbinic authorities had perforce to confirm one ruling as against the others. Whatever theory is accepted as pointing to the principle invoked for determining the authorized text, it can be argued that because of the fear that the objective study of discrepant biblical texts might produce more confusion, they evidently felt impelled to adopt a criterion which, while ruling out scholarly debate, was nevertheless decisive.

The Rabbis were not blind to the consequences which, in many instances, resulted from the application of whatever rule of selection they employed, whether by majority readings in their manuscripts or otherwise. It must have been obvious to them than an error in a parent manuscript would be reproduced by subsequent copyists and could thus become the reading most prevalent in manuscripts in use. They must have known that, by accepting certain readings through some arbitrary principle, they were actually perpetuating erroneous readings in the text. Such an unacceptable situation had to be remedied without, however, the need for making any alteration in the erroneous text they had to accept. This they did by drawing the attention of the reader to errors and directing that the corrections, which they supplied, were to be made *orally*. In the massoretic lists the formulae introducing such critical notes are (*a*) כְּתִיב - - - וּקְרִי, that is, '*the written word* [or words] is [or are] *to be read* (differently, as directed),' (*b*) כְּתִיב---וְלֹא קְרִי, that is, '*the written word is not to be read at all*', and (*c*) קְרִי - - - וְלֹא כְּתִיב that is, 'the word supplied is *to be read, though it is not written*', that is, 'the word missing in the text'. By insisting that no alteration in the authorized Hebrew text was ever to be made, even when a miscopying was evident and an oral correction was necessary, the Rabbis hoped that the sacred texts would be perpetually safeguarded. At the same time they made sure that where errors had become fixed in the text, the correct reading would nevertheless be made by the reader. It should be pointed out at this stage that only in medieval vocalized manuscripts and in the printed editions of the Hebrew Bible do massoretic notes appear. In Tora scrolls read in synagogue services there are no massoretic notes at all to attract the attention of the reader to errors and to their corrections. The reader is expected to be so familiar with his text that he should know when an oral correction of an error is to be made, without having any external aids to draw his attention to the error and the directed oral correction.

A perplexing feature in the rabbinic treatment of erroneous texts in the authorized Hebrew Bible is their ignoring of so many obvious errors, some of which will engage our attention in Chapter 4. We shall cite one instance where textual critics point to the same error occurring no less than three times in one verse, but the official rabbinic correction is confined to only one of these (pp. 38–40). Some explanation must be forthcoming to account for this strange phenomenon of restricted rabbinic selectivity in the identification and correction of scribal errors. One may hazard the suggestion that behind any correcting activity there lay the restraining influence of tradition. This possibility is hinted at by a debate in which the talmudic Rabbis were engaged on the question whether, in a consonantal text (that is, one without vowel-signs, as in a Tora scroll), the meaning of a word is to be determined by the context of the passage or whether the traditional vocalization (that is, with vowel-sounds) should prevail. This reference—in Sukka 6b—suggests the existence of a rabbinic tradition of readings in biblical texts. If this inference is plausible, one might tentatively suggest that where tradition supported the correction of an obvious error the correction was adopted. Where, however, the Rabbis had no tradition to support a correction, they felt that they had no option but to validate the disturbing word or phrase and perforce to infuse some sense into it by established interpretation. The restrictive influence of tradition would be in keeping with the rabbinic attitude, suggested earlier, in not enlisting scholarly study to determine readings to be validated, when discrepancies were manifested in biblical manuscripts.

From the foregoing it should not be concluded that the Massoretes confined their activities to providing a catalogue of faulty readings in the authorized Hebrew Bible and to their oral corrections. They also recorded variant traditional readings which, though not adopted in the official Hebrew Bible, were nevertheless considered worthy of note. Such variants are placed in a category designated by the Aramaic term נוּסְחָא אַחֲרִינָא. There are also lists of minor corrections under the heading of סְבִירִין '*S⁽e⁾bîrîn*'[1] relating mainly to grammatical adjustments, such as a singular verb being used where

---

[1] The term סָבִיר has been taken to mean 'conjecture'. However, the passive participle of this verb in talmudic language has the meaning of 'being of the opinion'.

a plural is required, e.g. the *S^eḇîr* note on the word וַיְהִי 'and was' in Numbers 9: 6 is וַיְּהִיוּ, 'and were' and on וַיָּבֹא 'and he came' in Numbers 13: 22 the *S^eḇîr* note is וַיָּבֹאוּ 'and they came'—the contexts in both instances requiring plural verbs. Occasionally an actual correction of the reading is made as, for example, in Exodus 14: 13 the words כִּי אֲשֶׁר 'for which' has the *S^eḇîr* note כִּי בַּאֲשֶׁר 'for as'. In the early consonantal text, in which vowel-letters had not been introduced, the spelling would have been כאשר, implying that the letter כ had been written once instead of twice (see pp. 58–60).

We must point out that, like the Massoreth, the scope of modern textual criticism is not restricted to the identification of textual errors in the biblical Hebrew texts and to attempts to recover the original words of the author or suggest a minor adjustment required by grammar. Discrepant readings representing different traditions become apparent when we compare readings in duplicated texts in the Hebrew Bible and compare readings in the Qumran texts, on the one hand, or renderings in the ancient versions, on the other hand, with those in the massoretic texts. Occasionally variant readings may imply nothing more than the choice of different words which do not in any way affect the sense of the line. There are instances, however, where variant readings do have different meanings and yet may all be admissible within the context of the passage. In such situations it may not be possible to justify the preference of one reading as against the other by the exercise of objective judgement. The textual critic may find himself in the same situation as the Massoretes and he may have to content himself simply with noting the alternatives without expressing any preference for one of the readings.

It should now be apparent that we are beginning to shape our presentation of modern textual criticism partly on a pattern which we find inherent in the rabbinic treatment of biblical texts. It would be appropriate, therefore, to give a summary outline of the two modes of handling biblical texts

by the talmudic Rabbis. These are designated by the terms
פְּשָׁט 'peshat' and דְּרַשׁ 'derash'. The former implies the 'plain
sense' of text which may be extended to restrained and sensible exegesis. The latter term, meaning 'inquiry', 'searching',
and so 'interpretation', allows for the free play of imagination
in exposition. Neither type of exposition was initiated by the
talmudic Rabbis, but both are much older. The objective
study of the Hebrew Bible reveals the interesting phenomenon
that there are interpolations in the text of notes which either
had been meant to be outside the text but were accidentally
incorporated into it by a copyist and are designated as glosses
(pp. 79 ff) or were attached to the text by the deliberate policy of the redactors and are thus recognized as editorial notes
(p. 89). We find that these observations bear the stamps of
both the *peshat* and   *derash* approaches and, as such, are not
to be attributed to the author. An analysis of such notes is in
itself important for the history of biblical exposition, particularly as they can be traced back, like scribal errors, to the
formative years of the Hebrew biblical text.

The *derash* system of exposition achieved impressive results
in two areas of rabbinic interest. In the sphere of pure homily
the Rabbis produced a volume of interpretations designed to
support moral teachings and embellish biblical folk-tales. They
also had a very practical motive in the appeal to the *derash*
mode of interpretation. The employment of an intricate system of casuistic interpretation of biblical texts provided them
with the biblical authority they sought for the validation of
their own religious and civil legislation. By this method of
exposition they authenticated their claim that (*a*) their own
devised regulations, along with those of their predecessors in
the chain of rabbinic tradition, were implicit in legal and even
in narrative and poetic texts of the Hebrew Bible, and (*b*)
only by the application of *derash* modes of interpretation
could the hidden extensions of the divine will inherent in
biblical texts be brought to light. Of course the texts thus
expounded were endowed with concepts never contemplated

by their authors, but the *derash* mode of exposition served their ends well. Where traces of such exposition are found incorporated in biblical texts they fall within the scope of textual criticism. However, when separated from the texts to which they became attached, they may be assembled into a body of what may be termed 'proto-rabbinic' literature.

Some of the talmudic Rabbis were alive to the fascination which might be exerted on the student by the *derash* system of exposition. They realized that, unless controlled, this kind of exercise could have the effect of obscuring, if not indeed supplanting, the plain sense of the text. They therefore insisted that a clear line of demarcation be made between these two modes of exposition and they warned the student to resist the temptation of presenting the *derash* results as the sense of the text intended by the author. This warning need not cause us any surprise, for there is an exact parallel today among those engaged in the devotional study of the Hebrew Bible. Sermons preached in synagogues and churches often have themes artificially associated with biblical texts by means of curious forms of interpretation. Like the *derash* expositors in talmudic times a modern preacher might feel justified in allowing himself unrestrained latitude in his exposition of a biblical text, in order to make it speak to some contemporary situation. Yet the cautionary note sounded by the talmudic Rabbis is as relevant today as it was in their time. While extravagant and forced interpretation of a biblical verse may be justified within its own restricted sphere of homiletics, this should never be presented as the true sense of the text expounded.

The talmudic caution against presenting the *derash* as the *peshat* is conveyed in explicit statements which could be taken as axioms. In the tractate Berakot 31b of the Babylonian Talmud we find the following pronouncement: דִּבְּרָה תוֹרָה כִּלְשׁוֹן בְּנֵי־אָדָם —'The Tora spoke in the language of ordinary men.' The reference here is to the phenomenon in Hebrew syntax of (what is described in grammatical works as) an infinitive absolute (but which in reality is a verbal noun) immediately preceding a finite verb with the effect of expressing emphasis. This statement warns the student that when he is confronted with what appears to him to be a strange grammatical formulation, he should not assume that some hidden information is thereby implied and that the significance of the implication involved is to be elicited by the application of a *derash* mode of interpretation. He is given a salutary reminder that the biblical writer employed ordinary language in his writing and that nothing more than plain sense was intended. While this pronouncement refers to the specific case mentioned in the above talmudic reference, we feel justified in regarding it as of general application. We feel that use was made of a current axiom and applied to a specific case. What is of special relevance to our introduction to modern textual criticism is that this axiom approximates the first basic assumption which the textual critic must make. That is, that the author of a given text wrote in a language and style meant to be intelligible to those for whom it was intended (p. 2).

The above rabbinic cautionary statement is reinforced by another, and more pointedly, pertinent axiom recorded in Sabbath 63a which states that אֵין מִקְרָא יוֹצֵא מִידֵי פְשׁוּטוֹ – 'a biblical text cannot lose [i.e. be deprived of] its plain sense.' Implied in this terse pronouncement is the stern warning that the *derash* method of exposition, though a useful tool legitimately employed for purely legal and homiletical purposes, must never be used so as to deprive the biblical text of its true, plain sense.

We now turn to an examination of the rabbinic directives to professional copyists, whose responsibility it was to produce accurate copies of the sacred texts. The Rabbis addressed themselves directly to this professional class, exhorting them to be ever vigilant against the accidental infiltration of errors into the texts they were preparing. Curiously, a general reminder of their special responsibilities is given in Sabbath 103b by way of a midrashic interpretation of the Hebrew word

וּכְתַבְתָּם 'and you shall write them', taken out of its context in Deuteronomy 6: 9. They playfully split this word into two, namely כְּתָב תָּם, meaning 'perfect writing', thereby indicating that, according to this hidden implication, the copyist is obliged by scriptural direction to produce a flawless copy of the biblical text he is preparing. Since there is no direct biblical reference to the need for meticulous care in the preparation of manuscripts of the sacred texts, the Rabbis felt obliged to resort to a midrashic exposition, in order to drive home their point with, apparently, scriptural authority. It does not really matter whether or not the Rabbis really believed that an exhortation was meant to be implied by the text. The midrashic method, like biblical folk-tales and parables, was an effective means of communicating their message. Their concern for the exact copying of biblical texts is further expressed in Megilla 18b that such work must not be done שֶׁלֹּא מִן הַכְּתָב, that is, 'without a written text' in front of the copyist. The copyist was forbidden to rely on his memory when engaged in the work of preparing a fresh copy of the sacred text, no matter how familiar he may have been with that text.

Following upon the general call for extreme care by the copyist, the Rabbis alerted them to the kind of errors to which they might be prone and against which they must be constantly vigilant. In the above quoted talmudic passage, Sabbath 103b, a list is given of groups of letters of similar appearance which could easily be confused by the copyist. These include א and ע, ב and כ, ד and ר, to quote but a few. Examples of textual corruption resulting from the confusion of letters of similar appearance are far from rare in the massoretic Hebrew Bible. Quite a number of these were corrected by the Rabbis, but we shall supply other instances of this type of error not cited by them to supplement the rabbinic list.

The Rabbis were also aware, as indeed are modern textual critics, that confused copying is not confined to letters of similar appearance. Words of similar appearance or sound may likewise to be confused. For example, the monosyllabic אֶל–'to' and עַל –'upon' are often confused in the massoretic text. An interesting example of such confusion which, incidentally, is not a hypothetical case as we shall demonstrate, is provided by the Mishna Sopherim V2. Practical advice is here given on how a faulty copying might be corrected by the copyist. The example given is that, if the copyist had intended writing the word יהוה (YHWH, that is, God's name) but unwittingly wrote instead the word יהודה (Yᵉhûḏâ–Judah), the remedy was very simple. All he had to do was to erase the terminal letter ה and then to convert the now terminal letter ד into a ה. However, if he had intended writing the name יהודה and instead wrote the divine name יהוה, the procedure for correcting this error was not very satisfactory. Since an alteration or erasion of any part of the divine name was regarded as sacreligious and therefore prohibited, the only way open to the copyist was to suspend a diminutive letter ד over the word, thus producing the inelegant form יהוᵈה.

A confusion between the two words יהודה and יהוה actually exists in the Hebrew text of 2 Samuel 1: 12. We are told that, following the receipt of the news of the death of Saul and his son Jonathan 'they mourned and wept and fasted till the evening for Saul and his son Jonathan and for *the people of the Lord* [עַם־יהוה in the massoretic text] and for the house of Israel which had fallen by the sword'. On general considerations one would say that the expression 'the people of the Lord' is out of balance with the later phrase 'the house of Israel'. One would conclude that something has gone wrong with the former expression. Turning to the *LXX* rendering, we find that the translation is actually τὸν λαὸν ʼΙούδα 'the people of Judah', representing the words עַם־יהודה. This is what we would have expected as the proper balance to the second expression.[2] We

---

[2] It appears that the federation of the tribes under Saul did not achieve a united monarchy but rather a dual monarchy. The two tribal groupings, Joseph (later Israel) and Judah, evidently retained their identities.

thus have an instance of where the copyist wrote the word יהוה instead of יהדה – the very example quoted by the Rabbis.

There are indeed a number of instances in the massoretic Hebrew Bible of a diminutive letter being suspended over a word with, it seems, the deliberate motive of altering the sense for some reason. Judges 18: 30 has such an example. In this passage we read that the Danites had set up an idol in their city and that a grandson of Moses called Jonathan and the latter's sons became priests to the tribe. The incident described in this passage was regarded as besmirching the memory of Moses, and to remove this embarrassing information the name מֹשֶׁה 'Moses' was changed to מְנַשֶּׁה 'Manasseh'. They used the device of suspending a diminutive נ over the consonantal word and thus produced the word מנשה. The fact that the *LXX* reading of this word is Manasseh, in accordance with the change made, points to the antiquity of this device. The medieval Jewish commentator Rashi, however, makes it plain that the diminutive letter over the word indicates that the readers were meant to understand that the reference was indeed to Moses.

As mentioned earlier, a divergence of rabbinic opinion is recorded in Sukka 6b on the question whether the consonantal text (without vowel-points) of the Hebrew Bible is the true guide to the correct understanding of the text or whether, alternatively, the traditional vocalization remains paramount. The fact that the majority view favoured reliance on the consonantal text is a telling rabbinic antecedent of modern textual criticism. When a vocalized (i.e. pointed) Hebrew word in a text presents a difficulty either in itself or in the light of the context, the textual critic will look at the word as it had been in its consonantal form before vowel-points had been attached. It might show the critic that the wrong vocalization had been applied to the word, since the context points to a different sense which indicates the appropriate vocalization and reading. One view is that in supplying the appropriate vocalization to replace the traditional one in the massoretic text, the critic is not really offering an emendation, since this procedure does not affect any change in the original, consonantal text. One may go a step further and say that since vowel-letters were not part of words in early texts but were introduced as an aid to reading, the removal of even vowel-letters does not constitute a change in the original, consonantal text. In such instances quite different words could emerge by the application of the appropriate vowel-letters or simply by none at all being attached. On the other hand, it could be argued that such critical procedures do constitute emendations, since the new meanings achieved thereby are different from those of the massoretic tradition. However, this difference in viewpoint does not affect the legitimacy of the critical attitude in removing not only the vowel-points, but even vowel-letters, in order to see the words as they were written in their earliest forms. It does not really matter whether such a procedure is explained as achieving an emendation or whether no alteration in the original text is effected.

3
THE SCOPE AND LIMITATIONS OF TEXTUAL CRITICISM

WE now turn to a general survey of the science of Textual Criticism, defining its scope and its limitations in biblical studies. The apparatus available to scholars for the critical study of the text of the Hebrew Bible consists mainly of the following elements:

1. The massoretic lists of oral corrections and other informational notes such as variant readings which, though rejected in the standardized Hebrew text, were nevertheless thought worthy of mention. Reference is occasionally made to medieval Hebrew manuscripts which represent two schools of the massoretic tradition, but the variant readings are generally of minor import.
2. The phenomenon of discrepant readings in duplicated passages or in parallel phrases within the Hebrew Bible.
3. The evidence of the ancient versions. By translating version renderings back into Hebrew it is often possible to see the readings which were before the translators.
4. Comparisons between readings in the massoretic Hebrew text with those in manuscripts of the same text found at Qumran (and generally known as the Dead Sea Scrolls), particularly in the complete text of Isaiah (designated by the siglum IQIs[a]).
5. The Samaritan Pentateuch, which is not a version but a recension of the Samaritan sect,
   and, to a minor extent,
6. The rules of parallelism in ancient Hebrew poetry.
7. Variant readings in manuscripts, collected by Kennicott and de Rossi (see bibliography). Though generally of a minor nature, these are nevertheless to be noted, even when the meaning of texts is unaffected by these variations.

We now consider each of the above items in the critical

apparatus, to indicate how each element may, where applicable, produce the kind of evidence required when the
critic is confronted with what is apparently a textual corruption. As pointed out earlier, the scholar will, in the first
place, attempt to understand a difficult text as it is. Only
when it becomes clear beyond any reasonable doubt that
corruption had been introduced into the text, will he apply
the critical apparatus at his disposal.

1. *Massoretic notes.* In the medieval Hebrew manuscripts
which have been preserved there are numerous massoretic
notes in the margins, while in the printed editions these are
relegated to the foot of pages. Most of these draw the attention of the reader to directed readings which are corrections
of scribal errors. We shall see in the next chapter that it is
possible to place these under separate categories of recurring
types of copyists' errors and that these categories are recognized by the modern textual critic.

However, when considering rabbinic directed adjustments
or substitutions or words or phrases in the Hebrew biblical
text, we must differentiate between what are presented as
corrections of faulty texts and those that are deliberate alterations made by them to avoid indelicate or theologically
unacceptable expressions. Eighteen such deliberate changes in
readings are listed by the Rabbis and are known as תִּקּוּנֵי סוֹפְרִים
tikkûnê sōpherîm; 'scribal emendations'. There are, however,
more instances of deliberate alterations in texts than the
recorded eighteen and those were made for the same reasons.
Though these are not in the rabbinic list, they may be recognized either from the evidence of an ancient version or even
from the context of the passage in which they occur. These
calculated alterations in readings in no way imply any kind of
textual irregularity or corruption. On the contrary, the literate
reader, being informed that the changes were made because
of religious scruple, realizes what the original words were. It
appears that no such scruples existed when the compositions
were made, that is when Hebrew was a living, spoken language

and had survived among the general populace as the language of the sacred texts and of prayer.

One of these *tikkûnê sōpherîm* appears in I Samuel 3: 13. In this text the sin of the two sons of the High Priest Eli, namely Hophni and Phineas, is described as מְקַלְלִים אֱלֹהִים 'they reviled, and showed contempt for God'. This kind of expression was evidently regarded by later generations as sacreligious and therefore objectionable, so that some substitution had to be made. They reduced the word אֱלֹהִים 'God' to לָהֶם 'for them (selves)'. Those who accepted the new reading were compelled to understand the sense of the phrase to mean something like 'they brought contempt upon themselves'. However, the rendering of the ancient Greek version, the Septuagint, κακολογοῦντες Θεόν 'speaking evil against God' represents the original Hebrew wording. The medieval Jewish commentator Kimhi informs his reader that here we have a תִּקּוּן סוֹפְרִים –a deliberate alteration in the text because of religious scruple.

In the prologue to the book of Job there are no less than four examples of the same euphemistic word being substituted for the one they thought to be objectionable, though these do not appear in any rabbinic list of substituted readings made for this reason. The author of the Prologue describes in vivid and dramatic language the trials which the unhappy Job had to endure at the instigation of Satan. They are verses 5 and 11 in chapter 1 and verses 5 and 9 in chapter 2. His children die, his fortune is lost, and he himself suffers unending agony from a painful skin eruption. Yet in spite of all his misfortunes and physical suffering Job refuses to relinquish his steadfast faith in God. His wife cannot bear to see his excruciating suffering and has no patience with his unfailing faith. In chapter 2, verse 9, she is represented as impatiently flinging the following words at him: 'Do you still hold fast to your integrity? Curse [or revile] God and die.' In the Hebrew text the word for 'curse', namely קַלֵּל was replaced by the one meaning 'bless', that is בָּרֵךְ. The expression 'curse God' was regarded as offensive if not, indeed, blasphemous: it was

therefore changed. In this instance (as in cases of *Tikkûnê
Sōpherîm*) the literate reader is expected to know the true
sense of the words attributed to Job's wife, even though the
key word had been replaced by another. While the scholar
will note this kind of phenomenon when it occurs, it will
readily be understood that such a change in reading does not
indicate an error due to miscopying. On the contrary, it indicates that there was no mistake at all in the text, but that it
was deliberately altered. The *LXX* rendering εἰπόν τι ῥῆμα
'say something against the Lord' is a euphemistic translation
of the original Hebrew. On the first occurrence of this substituted verb in Job 1: 5 in the expression וּבֵרְכוּ אֱלֹהִים בִּלְבָבָם –
'[perhaps] they blessed God in their hearts' for 'they showed
contempt for God', Ibn Ezra notes that here we have כִּינוּי – 'a
substitution' with the opposite meaning, while Rashi makes a
similar note. In the first three instances the Targum used the
Aphel, i.e. the causative, of the verb רְגַז which produced the
derived sense 'they angered' but this verb is used in the Targum of Leviticus 24: 11 to represent the Hebrew verb קִלֵּל with
the meaning of 'showing contempt for'.

Another case of deliberate alteration occurs several times
in the same word in Jeremiah 44, verses 17, 18 and 19, but
the change is achieved in a rather subtle way by altering the
vocalization of the word, thus producing an entirely different
word. In this passage the prophet castigates the people for
their practice of offering incense in the worship of idols (v. 5)
and he threatens them with dire divine punishment for their
apostasy. In response to this charge came the rather surprisingly defiant answer 'we will not listen to what you tell us in
the name of the Lord [v. 16]. We will fulfil all the promises
by which we have bound ourselves, burning incense למלכת השמים
[in the non-vocalized text of v. 17].' In the light of the context these two consonantal Hebrew words should be read as
לְמַלְכַּת הַשָּׁמַיִם 'to the queen of heaven'. The expression 'queen
of heaven', though false and absurd from the prophetic and
orthodox view, was nevertheless too blasphemous even to be

allowed to be mentioned, for it implied that in their turning to the nature religion of the nations around, the people had accepted the notion that Yahweh had a consort. The objectionable expression was ingeniously given quite a different meaning by the simple device of reading the first word differently, that is, by attaching a different set of vowel-signs. The Rabbis directed that it be read as לִמְלֶכֶת which was to be taken to mean 'the work of heaven' and, to make sure that the reader understood what the sense of the changed word is, the Massoretes added the note חָסֵר א׳ –'an א is missing'–the normal spelling of this word being לִמְלֶאכֶת. We do not have to rely solely on the context to see what the original word was. The *LXX* (in chapter 51 in the Greek arrangement of chapters) rendered it correctly τῇ βασιλίσσῃ 'to the queen'. The RSV, the JB, and the NEB translate the original word, as meant by the prophet.

The authorized Aramaic version, the Targum, representing the orthodox rabbinic standpoint, accepted the revised rabbinic vocalization and interpreted the expression to refer לְכוֹכְבַת שְׁמַיָּא 'to the stars of heaven'. Kimhi likewise accepted the rabbinic vocalization and remarked: 'the work of heaven denotes the stars, which are the handiwork of God.' It is, however, of relevance to observe that the Hebrew expression in the emended vocalization would have sounded strange and rather unnatural to an ancient Israelite. The noun used to denote something made or created is usually מַעֲשֶׂה from the root עָשָׂה 'did, made', while the word מְלָאכָה –the absolute form–normally refers to work in terms of activity or occupation. Furthermore, the use of the word שָׁמַיִם 'heaven' for 'God' is rabbinic rather than biblical, a fact which also points to rabbinic alteration. Once again this alteration in meaning brought about by the deliberate substitution of vocalization does not indicate any miscopying in the Hebrew text. Indeed, shorn of the rabbinic vocalization and restored to its original consonantal form, the text is perfectly correct, our function being to restore its proper vocalization and thus the sense intended by the author.

2. *Duplicated passages.* The following are some of the main duplicated texts in the Hebrew Bible: 2 Samuel 22 and Psalm 18, 2 Kings 18: 13-20: 11 and Isaiah 36: 1 – 38: 8, Psalms 14 and 53. Comparisons between these pairs of duplicated passages reveal many discrepant readings. Some of these are simply variant expressions which do not affect the sense of the lines, while others may be accounted for as scribal errors. These are discussed in Chapter 4, pp. 64–65.

3. *The Ancient Versions.* The two main ancient versions with which we shall be concerned are the Greek–the Septuagint usually designated as the *LXX*–and the Aramaic. The title of the ancient Greek version, the Septuagint, meaning seventy in Greek, derives from a certain 'letter of Aristeas' written about 150 BC in which he describes how King Ptolemy Philadelphus (265-240 BC) had requested a Greek translation of the Hebrew Scriptures and in response to his request seventy-two scholars were sent from Jerusalem to translate the Pentateuch into Greek for his royal library. In the course of time the title the 'translation of the Seventy', as it became loosely to be known, was used for the Greek version of the whole Hebrew Bible. The *LXX* version was made for the use of the Jewish population in the Greek-speaking city of Alexandria and was indeed begun in the third century BC. It began with a translation of the Pentateuch, while the other books of the Hebrew Bible were translated into Greek during that and the following century. It is thus the most ancient witness to a Hebrew recension which antedates the Qumran scrolls by about two centuries. There are many differences in readings between the massoretic Hebrew text and the one which lay before the Greek translators, but even allowing for discrepancies, the Hebrew text as a whole was faithfully translated. What is rather surprising is that some of the readings in the Qumran manuscripts support readings of the Hebrew text which the *LXX* translators had, as opposed to readings in the massoretic Hebrew text. Because of its antiquity the *LXX* was regarded by some textual critics as more trustworthy than the

massoretic Hebrew text, where discrepancies in readings occur. However, it is surely more prudent to treat each discrepancy separately, in the light of considerations which will be explained in examples given in Chapter 4.

Reference is occasionally made to the minor Greek translations. These are mainly known from the work of Origen (in 240-5 CE). Because of the many divergencies in manuscripts of the *LXX*, Origen produced what is termed a *Hexapla* edition consisting of six columns. These are the Hebrew text, a transliteration of the Hebrew words, the *LXX* itself, and the Greek versions of Aquila, Theodotian, and Symmachus. Aquila's version, known from the remnants of the Hexapla and from the Cairo Geniza, is interesting in that he often translates the Hebrew literally, thereby doing violence to the Greek language. According to Jewish sources he was a pupil of Rabbi Akiba and is even identified with Onkelos, the reputed author of the authorized Aramaic version of the Pentateuch.

Of the Aramaic versions, that of Onkelos on the Pentateuch is, in the main, faithful to the massoretic Hebrew text, with some exceptions mentioned below. The other Aramaic versions, the Palestinian and the one attributed to one Jonathan, follow the rabbinic midrashic pattern in representing unrestrained exposition which, in turn, reflects this form of rabbinic exposition. While in its present fixed form the Targum of Onkelos is rather late, its origins go back to pre-Christian times, when Aramaic was the vernacular. An Aramaic translation accompanied the reading of each verse of the Hebrew Scriptures in the synagogue service. In the oral stage the Aramaic renderings were, most likely, not uniform; standardization was later achieved when the Targum attributed to Onkelos became the recognized Aramaic version and was fixed in written form but, curiously, was no longer used in the synagogue service.

Reference should also be made to the Syriac version, called the 'Peshitta', meaning 'the simple'. It was produced probably in the second century CE and is generally faithful to the

Hebrew text, especially in the Pentateuch, but it occasionally betrays the influence of the *LXX*.

There are some limitations in the application of these ancient versions. Some discrepancies between readings in the Hebrew text and the renderings given by the ancient versions do not always point to different readings in the Hebrew text which lay before the translators. They may be accounted for by the different ways of expressing the same idea dictated by the modes of thinking in each language. Translators often find it impossible to produce a verbatim rendering of the Hebrew wording because of the nature of the language of the translation. Thus a word in the Hebrew text may be omitted in the *LXX* translation and, conversely, a word appearing in the Greek version may not be represented in the Hebrew text translated. We have only to think of parallel examples in the NEB to realize the truth of this phenomenon in translation. To quote but one of the many instances in which additional words occur in translation, Psalm 18: 42 (41) in the NEB reads 'They cry out and there is none to help them; *they cry* to the Lord and he does not answer.' The italicized words are not in the Hebrew text; they are not required by Hebrew usage and are, in fact, understood by the reader. However, because of the need evidently felt to make the point clear to English readers, the NEB translators added the extra words. One cannot resist the temptation to observe that, had this rendering appeared in the *LXX* version, some scholars would have seen in it evidence of words accidentally left out by the scribe of the Hebrew text. They would have indeed pointed out that the second half of the verse requires a word for 'crying out', as seen from the translation and would have argued for its restoration in the Hebrew text.

Occasionally translations in the ancient versions are modified because of theological scruples. The renderings of the *LXX* and the Targum on Exodus 24: 10 provide illustrations of this kind of deliberate change in the sense of a line. The Hebrew text tells us that 'they [i.e. Moses and those with him] saw the God of Israel'. The *LXX* interpreted this line to mean 'they saw *the place where* the God of Israel *stood* ', while the Targum rendered it to mean 'they saw *the glory of* the God of Israel'. Again, in the second half of this verse the text describes a pavement of sapphire 'under his [God's] feet', but the Targum, in order to avoid a possible anthropomorphic understanding, paraphrased or interpreted this to mean 'under his throne of glory'. Similarly, in Isaiah 38: 11 King Hezekiah says: 'I shall not see the Lord in the land of the living', but his statement is modified by the *LXX* version to mean 'I shall not see *the salvation of* the Lord . . .' and by the Targum to 'I shall not *appear before* the fear of the Lord in the land of the house of his presence'. In this latter example, though we know that the Targum on this passage in Isaiah imposed a circumlocutary type of interpretation on the line, what is of relevance here is that to avoid a theological dilemma posed by the direct sense of the line, the Targumist simply made the active verb 'I shall [not] see' into a passive 'I shall [not] be seen [i.e. appear] '. The *LXX* got over the difficulty by inserting the notion of the glory of God. In these passages the translators of the *LXX* and Targum had before them the same text as our massoretic recension. That their renderings deviate from the Hebrew reflects their religious scruples which inhibited any direct translation and motivated them to interpret the Hebrew words in terms of their own theological thinking. In such instances we note the modifications in the sense introduced by the translators of the *LXX* and the Targum and we understand their reasons for so doing. At the same time, we must stress that such deviations in meanings do not constitute examples of miscopying of the text in the Hebrew manuscript before translators, nor do they represent different readings which were in the Hebrew texts before them.

It is to be noted that while the Palestinian Targum and J generally represent the rabbinic interpretations of biblical texts, the Targum of Onkelos generally gives the plain sense of the text. Where, however, a rabbinic interpretation has a

practical effect on religious observance, Onkelos had no option
but to make his rendering conform with it. An example of
this is found in Leviticus 23: 11 and 15. The people are given
instructions about the presentation of the 'Omer'—a measure
of the first sheafs of the harvest—to the priest as God's rep-
resentative who, in turn, offers it to God on מִמָּחֳרַת הַשַּׁבָּת 'the
day following the Sabbath' (v: 11). On 'the day following the
Sabbath' they are to begin counting seven full weeks of fifty
days (vv. 15-16). The rabbinic interpretation of the expression
'the day following the Sabbath', as given in the Babylonian
Talmud, Tractate Menahot 65b—66a, is the day following the
first day of Passover. It may be that this interpretation was
motivated by the need to have the Feast of Weeks—Shavuot—
occur on a fixed, and not on a movable date. However that
may be, Targum Onkelos renders or, rather, interprets this
expression as מִבָּתַר יוֹמָא טָבָא 'the day following the Festival'.

Reference to the rules of parallelism in ancient Hebrew
poetry is sometimes relevant in any attempt to solve textual
difficulties in a biblical poetic composition. To appreciate its
relevance a brief description of what parallelism is will be useful here. Parallelism, a characteristic feature of ancient Hebrew
poetry, is a thought process whereby the parts of a poetic
verse are placed in forms of balanced ideas. To illustrate
what this definition means in actual poetic writing we select
from the Psalms three samples of the simplest types of parallelism. In each of these samples the verse consists of two
halves or stanzas. In Psalm 34: 2 we read 'I will bless the Lord
at all times; his praise shall always be in my mouth'. In this
verse the thought of the first half is repeated in the second,
but in different words. In Psalm 1: 6 is the statement that
'the Lord watches over the way of the righteous; but the way
of the wicked is doomed'. In this example the thought in the
second half stands in sharp contrast to that of the first. Our
third type is illustrated in Psalm 34: 18, which reads 'when
[men] cry out [for help] the Lord hears [them]; and he
delivers them from all their troubles'. Here the second half of

the line develops and rounds off the thought of the first half. The rules of parallelism, as briefly outlined here, could have some bearing on, and point to a solution of, a textual problem in a poetic composition in the Hebrew Bible. Once we have identified which form of parallelism the poet employed, an irregularity in one stanza may be remedied by reference to the thought in the other.

As mentioned earlier, one of the literary materials available for the critical study of the text of the Hebrew Bible is, in a restricted but nonetheless significant area, the complete Isaiah scroll of Isaiah of the Qumran cache. Its importance lies in the fact that it is 1,000 years older than any hitherto extant Hebrew manuscripts. When we compare this recension with the massoretic text we find that many of the standard types of scribal error are actually obvious in either tradition. In several instances, to which we shall draw attention, corrections were made in the Qumran scroll, most likely by another hand, sometimes to bring it into conformity with the massoretic text but otherwise to eliminate the copyist's errors. The main advantage of having the Qumran scroll is not that it has brought to light new facets of textual criticism, but that it provides visible examples of a variety of copyists' errors for the student clearly to see.

Having now dealt with the apparatus available for the critical study of biblical texts and having outlined its scope with its limitations, we now proceed to the next stage in our presentation. We find that the phenomenon of faulty readings in the massoretic Hebrew Bible is widely spread and recurrent. We can classify miscopyings into types of errors, of which the following are the main manifestations:

(*a*) The confusion of letters of similar appearance, and even of similar words, to which the talmudic Rabbis drew attention (p. 21). Such confusions are seen not only in our familiar square Hebrew script in use today, but also in the forms of the ancient Hebrew characters in which the original texts of the Hebrew Bible were written. For example, the letters ד

and ר may be confused in both scripts, their forms being ٥ and ٩ in the archaic script. On the other hand, ע and שׁ might be mistaken one for the other in our square script but, their forms in the ancient script being ο and ﭏ are not likely to be confused in this script. While a copyist is not likely to mistake a מ for נ or vice versa, they so closely resemble each other in the ancient script, being ﭏ and ﭏ, that they are thus likely to be confused.

(*b*) The accidental transposition of letters within a word.

(*c*) Evidence will be brought to show that in the earliest manuscripts as, indeed, in some discovered Hebrew inscriptions, there seems occasionally to have been no strict word division, so that the wrong division of a group of words, or groups of letters into words has sometimes been made by the copyist.

(*d*) Haplography, that is, the failure to repeat a letter or a group of letters in a word or words and, conversely,

(*e*) Dittography, or the accidental duplication of a letter or a group of letters in a word or words.

(*f*) Homoioteleuton—that is, when a word in a line occurs again in the next line and the copyist, having written that word in the first line, continues from that word in the next line, thus leaving out all the intervening words.

(*g*) The wrong vocalization of a correct consonantal text, due to a misunderstanding or to a divergent interpretation of the author's intent.

(*h*) Glosses. A gloss may be described as a brief note, often consisting of a single word which, evidently, was written above a word thought to need some elucidation and, consequently, meant to remain external to the text. Curiously, in the course of time, such explanatory notes were incorporated into the text by copyists (pp. 79 ff.).

A general observation about the types of errors given in the above classification is that most of them represent the kind of misreading or miswriting to which anyone making a copy of a literary composition is liable. The procedure which we shall adopt in the practical application of our apparatus of textual criticism will be simple and uncomplicated. We shall deal with each type of error successively under its own heading, identifying it in the first place, where possible, from a rabbinically directed oral correction. We shall then turn to texts in which the same type of error is recognized but is not on the list of rabbinic corrections. The identification of such an error is made possible by looking at this word as it appears in its correct form in a duplicated passage in the Hebrew Bible or by reference to renderings in the ancient versions which, when translated back into Hebrew, produce the correct reading. In situations where we cannot call upon external evidence, the context itself often points to the presence of the same kind of error. Once we have identified the type of error and can satisfactorily account for its occurrence in terms of ordinary human fallibility, we shall most likely be in a position to recover the original reading. Where, however, we cannot discover the nature of the miscopying and have to resort to conjecture, this exercise is not entered into lightly, but will be governed by considerations of context and the letters making up the words.

4

RECURRING TYPES OF ERROR

A. *Confusion of letters and even of words of similar appearance*

1. THE letters ד and ר (ᴀ and ᐟ in the archaic Hebrew script) are of similar appearance (in both scripts) and were liable to be misread and so miscopied one for the other by a copyist of a Hebrew biblical manuscript. 2 Kings 16: 6 provides an illuminating example of how this kind of copyist's error could lead to a confused and misleading account of a historical event. The preceding verse (5) informs the reader that 'Rezin, king of Aram, together with Pekah the son of Remaliah, king of Israel, came up to Jerusalem to wage war [against Ahaz, king of Judah] and they besieged Ahaz but they could not bring him to battle.' There is no difficulty with this plain statement but, in verse 6, the narrative in the massoretic Hebrew text (before rabbinic correction) continues with the information that 'at that time Rezin, king of Aram אֲרָם *restored* [the town of] Elath to Aram אֲרָם and he drove the Judahites out of Elath and the Arameans וַאֲרַמִּים came to Elath and have dwelt there to this day.' Now, in the first place, simple geographical facts make it plain that there is something wrong with this verse as it stands. The territory of Aram (modern Syria) lay to the north of Israel, whereas the town of Elath was at the head of what is now known as the gulf of Akaba and had been originally within the territory of Edom, which lay to the south-east of Judah. Furthermore, 2 Kings 14: 7 tells us that an earlier King of Judah, Amaziah, had conquered Edom and (in v. 22) that his son and successor Azariah had rebuilt Elath and restored it to Judah, presumably to ensure the freedom of the southern sea route from Judah. The talmudic Rabbis, who were familiar with the geography of the area now known as the Fertile Crescent and perhaps bearing in mind the information of the capture and the rebuilding of Elath as recorded in

chapter 14, realized that in 2 Kings 16: 6 it must have been the Edomites, and not the Arameans, who had reoccupied Elath. They therefore directed that the (consonantal) word וארמים should be read (orally) as ואדמים and pointed וַאֲדוֹמִים 'and the Edomites'. They thus indicated that, in their view, the letter ד had been misread, and so miscopied, as a ר by a copyist. We shall offer a reasonable explanation of this particular error below (p. 40).

This single massoretic correction does not resolve the confused account of the military reverse suffered by the Judahites in this campaign. As the text now stands the statement is made that Elath was *restored* to the far-away kingdom of Aram, implying that it had formerly been, if not within the Aramean territory, at least under its jurisdiction. It is argued that since the above-mentioned massoretic correction is valid, the second mention of ארם ('Aram') should likewise be restored to אדם and pointed אֱדוֹם 'Edom'. At this stage of textual restoration the narrative would tell us that Elath, which had earlier been an Edomite town, was restored to their original inhabitants, the Edomites. The account, however, is still not free from difficulty. The situation now presented is that Rezin, king of Aram, having an idle army besieging Jerusalem, marched to the extreme south, conquered Elath, and magnanimously handed it back to the Edomites. It is more likely that the Edomites, taking advantage of Ahaz's helpless and critical position in his besieged Jerusalem, seized the opportunity to attack the Judahites occupying Elath, drove them out, and regained the town themselves. It follows logically, then, that the leader of this Edomite military expedition had been the king of Edom and not the king of Aram, so that the first mention of אֲרָם should also be emended to its original אֱדוֹם. In reply to a possible objection that it could nevertheless have been Rezin, the king of Aram, who conquered Elath, a summary account of the facts is given in 2 Chronicles 28: 17 to the effect that following Ahaz's appeal to the Assyrians for help (v. 16), 'the Edomites came and defeated Judah and took captives'.

We thus reach the conclusion that in 2 Kings 16: 6 there is a triple error in reading אֲרָם for אֱדוֹם and that the Massoretes only restored one of these correct readings. We suggest that the first misreading of the word אֱדוֹם as אֲרָם was due to the reference to the king of Aram in the preceding case and this, in turn, precipitated the two subsequent misreadings. Having before him the opening words 'at the time the king of Aram restored Elath ....', the reading established in the text, a subsequent editor identified this king of Aram as Rezin who, as reported in the preceding verse 5, had laid seige to Jerusalem in alliance with Pekah, king of Israel. We may now claim that the true text of 2 Kings 16: 6 reads: 'At the time [that is, while Ahaz was helplessly besieged in Jerusalem by Rezin and Pekah] the king of Edom restored Elath to Edom, and he drove the Judahites out of Elath and the Edomites came to Elath and they have dwelt there to this day.' We have gone to some length in working out the solution of this textual difficulty, in order to show how much a simple misreading of a letter can confuse and distort an historical account. A further motive has been to provide an illustration of how a faulty text may be corrected by identifying the type of error involved and explaining its intrusion in terms of human misunderstanding or fallibility. Finally, by eliminating the error, we have shown how the true text may be restored.

The textual critic will not stop at this rational restoration, for he will point to the curious fact that the official Aramaic version, the Targum, retained the $k^e t\hat{\imath}b$, i.e. the written, uncorrected word וַאֲרַמִּים which is rendered faithfully as וַאֲרָמָאֵי 'and the Arameans'. Does this retention of the $k^e t\hat{\imath}b$ in the Targum point to a tradition different from the massoretic or, alternatively, to a certain independence based on an interpretation of the verse in the light of its context?

The critic will, furthermore, point to other similar instances of a misreading of the letter ד as a ר, two of which are to be found in 2 Samuel 8: 12 and 13. In the former verse reference is made to the spoils taken from *Aram,* Moab, and Ammon while, in the parallel passage in 1 Chronicles 18: 11 the three nations are listed as *Edom*, Moab, and Ammon, the three territories which lay immediately to the east of the Jordan. Again, in the narrative of 2 Samuel 8: 13 David is reported as having defeated *Aram* in the valley of Salt, whereas the same account in 1 Chronicles 18: 12 states that it was *Edom* that David's general, Abshai, had defeated. The error in the text of 2 Samuel 8: 12-13 may be accounted for by the copyist's mistakenly associating the campaign in this passage with the earlier one in verses 5 and 6 of this chapter, in which David is said to have defeated Aram and made it a vassal state. By way of a footnote it may be added that, in 1 Samuel 21: 8 and 22: 9 the warrior Doeg is said to have been an Edomite (אֲדוֹמִי). whereas the *LXX* describes him as ὁ Σύρος 'the Syrian', the later Greek term for Aramean. In this instance the *LXX* read the consonantal Hebrew word אדמי as אֲרָמִי, that is, reading a ר for a ד.

An intriguing historical problem is posed by the *LXX* rendering of a line in 1 Samuel 17: 8 involving the confusion of the letters ד and ר in a word. In this passage the Philistine giant Goliath arrogantly and defiantly hurls a challenge, apparently at the Israelites, that they should choose a champion to do single combat with him and that the issue of victory on the national scale should be decided on the result of this combat. In the course of his tirade Goliath is represented in the massoretic text as declaring, 'Surely I am a Philistine (אֲנִי הַפְּלִשְׁתִּי) and you are servants of Saul (וְאַתֶּם עֲבָדִים לְשָׁאוּל).' On general considerations one might have expected the statement in the second half of the line to have designated the Israelites as an ethnic entity to balance his description of himself as a Philistine if, indeed, his challenge was hurled at the Israelites. Turning to the *LXX* rendering of this latter expression, we find καὶ ὑμεῖς Ἑβραῖοι τοῦ Σαούλ 'you are Hebrews of Saul', representing the Hebrew reading וְאַתֶּם עֲבְרִים לְשָׁאוּל In recognizing that we have here an obvious confusion between the Hebrew letters ד and

ר (i.e. between the readings עבדים and עברים),we ask 'Which reading is appropriate to the context?'

The clue to the answer of this question may be provided by the following considerations. Firstly, the word עִבְרִים usually translated 'Hebrews', was never used by the Israelites in the biblical narrative to designate themselves as a people. Secondly, some scholars hold that this Hebrew term corresponds to the Babylonian word *Habiru* and that this Babylonian word did not denote an ethnic group but bands of rootless people who roamed over the Fertile Crescent from about 2000 BC till some time in the eleventh century BC. Thirdly, the way of life of the Habiru was that when a battle was impending or actually in progress, they would hire themselves as mercenaries to one of the contending armies. If the *LXX* rendering represents the original reading of the Hebrew text, then the following deductions may be made. As the Philistines and the Israelites were poised for the crucial battle to determine which of the two nations would win mastery of the country, a third force, namely the Habiru, appeared on the scene, as we might have expected. Both sides must have realized that the added weight of the Habiru would most likely secure victory for the side they joined. If the original Hebrew text had the reading 'you are Habiru attached to Saul', it could follow that the Habiru had joined Saul's army. Goliath's taunt, then, was directed not to the Israelites but to the Habiru, with the aim of detaching them from the Israelites and persuading them to join the Philistines. If this reconstruction of the military situation before the battle is correct, then we would be entitled to say that, with the aid of the *LXX* rendering, we restore the original reading of the Hebrew text and, at the same time, recover a lost page of early Israelite history. On the other hand, the term עִבְרִים *Ibrīm* was applied to the Israelites by the Philistines in the narrative of 1 Samuel as a designation of contempt as, for example, in 14: 11, 'The Philistines said "The *Ibrīm* are coming out of the holes where they were hiding." '
If the reading indicated by the *LXX* is correct, it could be

argued that it suggests nothing more than the contemptuous term used by the Philistines to designate the Israelites. Whichever view is taken, there is at any rate a confusion between these two letters of similar appearance. The argument in favour of the proposed historical reconstruction is the presence of the word לְשָׁאוּל

Following these two examples involving historical data, we cite an example of this kind of scribal error which introduced a distortion into the text, thus making it unintelligible. Our reference is Joshua 6: 18. In this passage the narrator tells us that, as the confederation of Hebrew tribes under the military leadership of Joshua was about to unleash an assault on the city of Jericho, the people were warned not to appropriate to themselves anything from the spoils of the city when it fell to their attack. The verse in question reads: 'you must keep yourselves [away] from the devoted things פֶּן תַּחֲרִימוּ *lest you make [it] devoted* and you take from the devoted things'. This awkward phrase, underlined in the English translation, is quite unintelligible. Turning, however, to the *LXX* version we find μήποτε ἐνθυμηθέντες 'lest you set your mind upon'. When we translate the Greek back into Hebrew, we find that it expresses the meaning of Hebrew words פֶּן תַּחְמְדוּ 'lest you covet, you wish to acquire'. This is the sense required by the context and given in JB and NEB. Thus the copyist wrote (in the consonantal text) the word תחרמו instead of תחמדו, thereby not only misreading the ד as a ר but also transposing the letters מר. It is not satisfactory merely to point out the scribal error; one must attempt to account for it. It seems that the copyist seeing the word חרם before and after this word, took this word to be a verbal form of the same noun חרם The error was not simply due to a misreading of the eye but, it appears, the misreading was brought about by a mistaken interpretation of the sense meant to be conveyed by the writer.

We now turn to the complete Isaiah scroll from Qumran for examples of the confusion between the Hebrew letters ד and ר Verse 14 of Chapter 16 ends with the statement that the glory of Moab will be brought into contempt and that those who survive would be 'without strength'—לֹא כַּבִּיר in the massoretic text. The Isaiah scroll, however, has the reading ולוא כבוד 'without honour'. Was the copyist influenced by this word in the line above or does this reading suit the context better? This is the reading underlying the *LXX* rendering οὐκ ἔντιμος—'not honoured'. Here the judgement of the scholar will be brought to bear on this issue. In the consonantal text (without vowel-signs or vowel-letters) the word כבר in the massoretic recension was read as כבד (that is, כָּבוֹד) in the Qumran recension. Similarly, the expression מים כבירים, 'mighty waters' of 17: 12 in the massoretic text is found as מים כבדים 'heavy waters', in the Qumran text; it was probably understood in the sense of the great pressure of the water. Looking at the text in its earlier consonantal form without vowel-letters we see that the copyist read כבדם for כברם. Again in 42: 13 the massoretic reading יריע 'he will shout aloud', appears in the Qumran text as יודיע, 'he will make known'. In the consonantal text ירע was copied as ידע In 33: 8 the massoretic text reads: 'Covenants are broken, cities עָרִים are despised.' One immediately notes that the rejection of cities does not balance with the breaking of covenants. The Qumran text, however, read עדים (עֵדִים) meaning 'witnesses are despised'—a phrase which fits the context well and is to be adopted as the true reading—another example of misreading a ד as a ר in the massoretic text.

2. ה and ח (ᛏ and Ħ in the archaic Hebrew script) are similar in appearance and in sound and so lend themselves occasionally to be misread one for the other. A massoretic correction of a name in 2 Samuel 13: 37 provides a simple, though unimportant, example of this kind of confusion. The name of the father of a certain Talmai, king of Geshur (with whom Absalom sought refuge after the murder of his half-brother Amnon), is given in the *k*e*tîb* as עַמִּיחוּר, *Amîḥûr* but corrected by the Massoretes to עַמִּיהוּד, *Amîhûd* as in the *LXX*. According to this alteration not only was the ד read as a ר but also the ה

as a ח. An instance where the sense of the line has been altered through this kind of misreading is found in Proverbs 9: 1. The verse reads 'Wisdom has built her house; she has hewn out חָצְבָה her pillars seven'. One would say that the hewing out of the pillars should have preceded the work of building a house and not followed it. However, the Targum rendering עַתְּדַת and the *LXX* ὑπήρεισε, both meaning 'she set up', are translations of the Hebrew הִצִּיבָה. This recovered Hebrew word is a satisfactory parallel to בָּנְתָה 'she built' in the first half of the verse and is adopted in the translations of the RSV, the JB, and the NEB. When we write this word in its early consonantal form (before the introduction of vowel-letters and vowel-signs) it is הצבה we can thus readily see how the copyist misread the initial letter ה as a ח and so vocalized it as חָצְבָה.

3. A ז and ו(ץ and ד in the archaic Hebrew script) are of similar appearance and liable to be confused. The example we cite is in 1 Samuel 14: 47, where the narrator's enthusiastic account of Saul's extraordinary military prowess ends with these words וּבְכֹל אֲשֶׁר יִפְנֶה יַרְשִׁיעַ. The RSV, following earlier interpretations of the sense of the last word, translated this line as 'wherever he turned, he put [them, i.e. his enemies] to worse'. The difficulty about this last Hebrew word is that the verbal root (רשע) generally denotes a moral or judicial judgement and not defeat in battle. However, the solution to this textual difficulty is supplied very simply by reference to the rendering of the *LXX* ἐσώζετο representing the Hebrew יִוָּשַׁע. This Niphal (passive) form of the verb ישע (ושע) generally means 'he was saved' but, in a military context, its meaning is 'he was victorious'. This recovered Hebrew reading suits the context admirably, the full line now meaning 'wherever he turned he was victorious'. The JB adopts this restored word, but the NEB rendering 'wherever he turned he was successful' does not convey the precise sense conveyed by the restored Hebrew word, for it does not have regard for the military context of the narrative.

B. *The accidental transposition of letters within a word.*
This kind of miscopying is another manifestation of human
fallibility and we cite two examples by way of illustration.
The first one occurs in 1 Samuel 14: 27. The narrative preceding this verse deals with the strategy employed by Saul
in a battle between the Israelites and the Philistines. To
ensure divine support he invoked a solemn ban against the
eating of any food till complete victory was achieved. His
son Jonathan who, at the time of Saul's proclamation, was
absent on a special military assignment, was not aware of
the ban and, coming across a wild honeycomb, he dipped his
staff into it and, by tasting the honey, his flagging energy was
revived. His restoration of energy is described by the narrative
in these words–וַתָּאֹרְנָה עֵינָיו–'his eyes *brightened*'. The copyist of what became the massoretic text, however, misread this
word in its consonantal form as ותראנה instead of ותארנה with
the meaning (of וַתִּרְאֶנָּה) 'and his eyes *saw*'. Because of
the frequent association of 'seeing' with the mention of 'eyes',
the copyist, in his mind and so in writing, transposed the
letters אר to רא. The Massoretes directed that the restoration
of the correct word be made by the reader orally. The *LXX*
rendering ἀνέβλεψεν–'he recovered his sight', seems to represent the Hebrew *K^e tîb*. That the massoretic restoration is
correct is proved by the recurrence of this root in verse 29,
in which Jonathan says אֹרוּ עֵינָי–'my eyes brightened'.

Our second example of the transposition of letters within
a word, leading to the distortion of the true sense, appears in
Psalm 49: 12. The poet comments on the folly of men who
accumulate wealth, since it will not accompany them in death.
He reminds such people that קִרְבָּם בָּתֵּימוֹ לְעוֹלָם a line which is
wholly unintelligible. The AV awkwardly interpreted this line
to mean 'their inward [thought is that] their habitations [will
endure] for ever'. This paraphrasing apparently follows the
comment of the medieval Jewish commentator Rashi that
'their plans are to build for themselves houses which will
endure for ever'. Clearly this text was found to be perplexing

by Rashi and the AV translators and they were forced to have recourse to interpretation. However, this difficulty is easily resolved by reference to the *LXX* rendering of the first word, which is τάφοι, meaning 'graves'. The parallel translation of the Aramaic Targum בֵּית קְבוּרְתְּהוֹן 'their burial chambers or cemetaries', with the *LXX* rendering τάφοι, point to an original קְבָרָם 'their grave or tomb in their eternal home'. We thus have another instance of the copyist transposing two letters within the one word. The medieval Jewish commentator Ibn Ezra, who was noted for his more rational approach to the text of the Hebrew Bible, observed that 'there are those who say that קרבם is a reversal (הֶפֶךְ) of the word קברם.' This simple restoration of the transposed letters in this word makes the thought of the poet clear and consistent with his theme. He declares rather cynically that it is not wealth but the grave which lasts for ever. The talmudic Rabbis seem to have been uncomfortably aware of this unfortunate distortion which had become established in the text but, as suggested earlier (p. 16), perhaps having no warrant from tradition to direct the required oral correction, they left in the text unaltered. Nevertheless, they obliquely drew attention to this error, using a well-tried midrashic formula. In the Babylonian tractate *Moed Katan* 9b there is a homiletic comment on this line which states 'do not read קרבם but קברם'. While a purely homiletic intent is indicated by the employment of the formula אל תקרי אלא —'do not read [the word in the text] but [a modification suggested]—one cannot escape the conclusion that they were aware of the true reading of this Psalms line but they had not the authority to restore it.

The verb נָעְתַּם[1] in Isaiah 9: 18 (followed by אֶרֶץ) and meaning '[the earth] is scorched' is found in The Qumran scroll as נתעם and in 40: 20 the verb יִרְקַב 'will rot' is found as ירבק in the Qumran scroll. Both readings in the Qumran scroll are unintelligible. In 14: 31 the transposition of letters in the

---

[1] This word is obscure in any case, but even if the meaning attached to it is not certain, we have here an example of a copyist's transposition of letters in a word.

Qumran text produced a sense at variance with that of the massoretic text. The latter reads 'there is no straying בְּמוֹעֲדָיו', meaning 'in his ranks'. This was copied in the Qumran scroll as במודעיו, which would be read as בְּמוֹדָעָיו 'among his friends'.

C. *Wrong division of groups of letters into words*

From the following and other examples it seems that, in the very early manuscripts, there was no strict division of words; it looks as if, in some instances at any rate, the lettering ran in a continuous line. It is not to be marvelled at, therefore, that a copyist could be led into the wrong divisions of words when he misunderstood or misinterpreted the intent of the author. An illustration of such a phenomenon is found in the concluding words of Psalm 42: 6. This whole verse is a refrain which is repeated, in the correct form, at the end of Psalms 42 and 43 (leading some scholars to regard the two Psalms as originally one). The expression is יְשׁוּעֹת פָּנַי וֵאלֹהָי, literally, '[he, i.e. God, is] the salvation of my face and my God', the sense of which seems to be 'he is my deliverer . . .' When we turn to what has happened to this line at the end of verse 6 and continued into verse 7 we find it to be יְשׁוּעֹת פָּנָיו (v. 6) אֱלֹהַי (v. 7): 'the salvation of his face: O my God . . .' A reasonable explanation of this distortion is that the copyist had before him the undivided writing ישעתפניואלהי and, while having no difficulty in separating the first word from the second, he wrongly divided the second and third words after the letter ו instead of after the preceding letter י. He was now left with the isolated word אֱלֹהַי 'my God' and had no option but to place it at the beginning of the next verse. Since no verse followed the other two occurrences of the refrain at the end of each Psalm, this confusion did not take place. It is curious that the *LXX* version of this phrase (which is 41: 5 in the *LXX*) follows the wrong massoretic word division, except that it is also read פָּנַי in this instance, evidently to maintain consistency with the wording in the refrain of the other two verses. The Targum, on the other hand, not only adhered to the wrong word division in verse 6 but read פָּנָיו 'his face' in all three places. In this example the repeated refrain at the end of both Psalms points to the correction of the faulty word division at the end of verse 6.

We next cite Hosea 6: 5 for a further example of wrong division of letters into words. The prophet, as God's spokesman, makes the following statement: 'Therefore I have hewn them down through my prophets, I have slain them by the word of my mouth' וּמִשְׁפָּטֶיךָ אוֹר יֵצֵא which, as it stands, means 'and thy judgements, light goes forth'. Clearly this last part of the verse is a confused text. Even if we were to consider the word מִשְׁפָּטֶיךָ as an example of the objective use of the pronominal suffix and take it to mean 'The judgements [i.e. the verdicts or punishments] against you', we would still a prepositional prefix in the next word אוֹר. When, however, we turn to the *LXX* and the Targum versions, we find their renderings respectively to be καὶ τὸ κρίμα μοῦ ὡς φῶς ἐξελεύσεται and וְדִינִי כִּנְהוֹר נָפַק, both of which mean 'and *my* judgement goes forth like the light'. When translated back into Hebrew the phrase reads וּמִשְׁפָּטִי כָּאוֹר יֵצֵא. When reconstructing the consonantal, apparently undivided, letters of the early text, namely משפטיכאור, we see that the copyist wrongly attached the letter כ to the end of the first word as a pronominal suffix, whereas it properly belongs to the beginning of the second word as a prepositional prefix. The RSV follows this restored correct reading. The JB and NEB place this phrase after the first stanza in verse 3 and read מִשְׁפָּטוֹ 'his justice', i.e. God's justice. Our concern here is the correct reading of the parent of the massoretic text as it was in the original undivided sequence of letters.

A third example of the wrong division of a group of letters into words is furnished by Jeremiah 23: 33. The massoretic text reads as follows: 'When this people or a prophet or a priest asks you "What is the burden of the Lord['s oracle]?", then you shall say to them אֶת־מַה־מַשָּׂא' which is grammatically untenable and which some translators took to mean 'What burden?' It certainly perplexed the Targum translator, for all he could do was to offer the interpretation כְּדֵין נְבוּאָתָא 'thus is the prophecy of the Lord'. The LXX rendering, however, ὑμεῖς ἐστε τὸ λῆμμα 'you are the burden of the Lord['s oracle]' represents the original Hebrew אַתֶּם הַמַּשָּׂא. This makes very good sense, being the answer the prophet gave to the theoretical question. When we put the letters of these words of the massoretic text back into their consonantal form without any marked word division, we see that the copyist probably had before him אתמהמשא. Instead of dividing them into the two words he wrongly divided them into three words and thereby introduced a corruption into a perfectly good text. The examples quoted above point to one of the methods the textual critic employs when faced with an enigmatic text. He will reproduce the original, undivided wording of the text to see whether the copyist had made a wrong division of the continuous writing into words.

In the massoretic text of Isaiah 30: 5 the opening words are, in the $k^e t\hat{\imath}b$, כֹּל הִבְאִישׁ, which could mean 'everything, or every one, he has made tò stink [i.e. loathsome]' and this was altered by the Massoretes to read כֹּל הוֹבִישׁ 'everyone has come to shame'—the $k^e r\hat{e}$—the word to be read for the written one. The Qumran text had the same lettering as the massoretic $k^e t\hat{\imath}b$, except that the division of the letters into words was different, being כלה באש, read as כֻּלֹּה בָּאַשׁ and meaning 'everything, or every one, stinks [i.e. is loathsome]'.

The above examples are simple and uncomplicated, but sometimes the failure of a copyist to make the correct division of a continuous writing into the appropriate words may lead to a further corruption in a word or phrase. The end of the verse in Ezekiel 26: 20 is a case in point. The prophet, speaking as God's medium of communication, describes the downfall of the city of Tyre in these terrible words: 'I will make you dwell in the netherworld, in places long desolate, with those who go down into the pit, so that you shall not again be inhabited וְנָתַתִּי צְבִי בְּאֶרֶץ הַחַיִּים', which, as the phrase stands, can only mean 'and I shall set beauty in the land of the living'.

It is obvious that this last phrase is completely out of keeping with the context and that something went wrong in the copying. When we turn to the Targum translation we see that the translators experienced difficulty in understanding this enigmatic phrase. They resorted to a midrashic interpretation and gave the sense as 'I will give *joy* in the land of *Israel*'. The forced identification of 'the land of the living' with 'the land of Israel' interprets the intent of the oracle to be that, while Tyre will be annihilated, Israel, by contrast, will enjoy happiness. However, the *LXX* rendering gives us the clue to the recovery of the original words and, so, of the prophet's message. It translated the first two words as μηδὲ ἀναστῆς which, when translated back into Hebrew, read וְלֹא תִתְיַצְּבִי 'you [Tyre] will not take your place' in the land of the living. This statement admirably follows and completes the description of the fate of Tyre given in the preceding part of the verse. How, then, can we explain the distortion introduced into this line? When we write down the original words in the consonantal, undivided sequence of letters, what the copyist saw was ולאתתיצבי . It looks as if he wrongly identified the last three letters as the word צְבִי 'beauty' and the combination of the preceding three letters תתי as defective for the familiar word נָתַתִּי. There remains the negative which he omitted and one can only assume that he must have considered this as a corruption which he eliminated.

In 1 Samuel 9: 1 the Massoretes rightly drew the attention of the reader to the accidental splitting of the word מִבִּנְיָמִין ('from Benjamin') into the two words מִבֶּן יָמִין (the $k^e t\hat{\imath}b$) in the received text. On the other hand, in Psalm 123: 4 they unnecessarily split the word לַגְּאָיוֹנִים 'to proud [men]' into two words לִגְאֵי יוֹנִים 'to the proud oppressors'. The text with the undivided word, in speaking of 'the contempt of proud [men]' presents no difficulty whatsoever and, in fact, is in keeping with the first half of this half-verse which speaks of 'the scorn of those who are at ease'. To explain the massoretic directive that this word should be read as two, we would have to postulate the view that their understanding of the expression had been based on a traditional interpretation which saw in the conduct of proud men the character of oppressors.

In contrast to the phenomenon of textual corruption resulting from the splitting of words there are instances in the Hebrew biblical text of the reverse process having taken place. That is to say that the copyist failed to divide a group of continuous letters into the words required by the context of the verse and he thereby created a textual corruption in the text. An excellent example of this type of error is found in Psalm 89: 45. The first half of the verse reads הִשְׁבַּתָּ מִטְּהָרוֹ which is taken to mean 'Thou [God] has made his purity to cease' is, firstly, unintelligible and, secondly, out of balance with the second half which reads 'and thou hast hurled his throne to the ground.' To deal with the disturbing prepositional prefix מ 'from', some translators have followed the medieval commentator Ibn Ezra in reading the word as a nominal form מִטְהָר, with a slight modification in pointing, on the basis of the noun מִקְדָשׁ 'sanctuary'. Rashi takes the noun 'purity' to have the extended sense of 'brightness' and cites as evidence the analogy of this noun in the form טֹהַר in Exodus 24: 10. He argued that, since in the Exodus context this noun is descriptive of heaven, it must denote the notion of 'brightness'. Even if one were to concede this far-fetched line of argument, the problem still would remain that the expression thus interpreted is out of balance with what follows. To resolve this problem it is necessary firstly to rewrite this enigmatic word in its original consonantal form, which is מטהרו. We now see that this group of letters should have been divided into two words (מטה הודו) and that the letter ר was a misreading of the letter ד. We now have the restored reading הִשְׁבַּתָּ מַטֵּה הוֹדוֹ 'Thou hast caused his glorious sceptre to cease' and this balances well with the succeeding words 'Thou hast hurled his throne to the ground'. Once the copyist misread the two words as one, he saw in it the word מטהרו.

In Isaiah 22: 5 the massoretic text reads מְקַרְקַר קִר וְשׁוֹעַ אֶל־

הָהָר which could mean 'battering down the walls and a shout-
ing to the mountains'. This is a rather difficult line, so that
some scholars would read וְשׁוֹאָה instead of וְשֹׁעַ with the sense
'destruction'. Whatever the true meaning may be, it is clear
that the consonantal text, as read by the Massoretes, was שוע.
In the Qumran recension we find the single word קדשו 'his
holiness' for קיר ושוע; this, most likely, was understood to refer
to the Jerusalem Temple. It is to be noted also, as will be
shown later (pp. 67–68), that the letter ע had evidently lost its
consonantal, guttural sound, and was not heard in some words
containing this letter, so that the word שוע could easily have
been pronounced, and therefore written, שו[2]. The Qumran
text, then, when compared with the massoretic text, provides
an example of the fusing of two words into one in the consonantal forms of the words without vowel-letters and, at the
same time, of misreading a ר as a ד—קרשו into קדשו.

D. *Dittography, the accidental duplication of a letter or letters*
in a single word or group of words in the massoretic biblical
text.

In the Babylonian talmudic tractate Nedarim 37b-38a a list
of dittographies is given under the heading הלין כתיבן ולא קריין
'these [words, though] written [in the Hebrew text] are not
to be read', that is, they are to be omitted in reading. A clear
example of dittography appears in Jeremiah 51: 3, where the
word ידרך had been accidentally repeated. In the printed,
pointed editions of the Hebrew Bible in use today, the duplicated word is printed without any vowel-points. The attention of the reader is thus drawn to the presence of the error,
which he finds corrected in the footnote כתיב ולא קרי 'it
is written, but is not to be read.' If the reader had this text
before him in a handwritten scroll, he would be expected to
know that this word had been unwittingly duplicated and to

---

[2] We shall later cite instances in the Qumran complete scroll of Isaiah where the
letter ע was omitted and restored above the word, most likely by another hand. In
fact, the name of the prophet יְשַׁעְיָהוּ is found at the beginning of chapter 1 as
ישׁיהו

omit it in reading. Even without the intrusion of the dittography the line is difficult and the meaning obscure. As it
would not be helpful to go beyond our main purpose, which
is to point to an unmistakable incident of a dittography, we
refer the student to the standard critical works on the book
of Jeremiah.

A similar example of the sheer accidental duplication of
a word is found in the Qumran Isaiah scroll, 31: 6. The
massoretic text reads (with a slight emendation) 'Return to
the one [i.e. God] —לַאֲשֶׁר–from whom you have so deeply
turned aside'. The Qumran text reads לאשר לאשר, a clear case
of accidental dittography.

To illustrate that the tendency towards dittography in the
copying of biblical texts was more widespread than the offical
rabbinic notes suggest, we list a few not noted by them, which
we correct either by reference to the ancient versions or by
indications in the text itself. In Ezekiel 28: 23 we have an
example of the accidental duplication of a single letter in a
word, leading to a distortion of the sense. The prophet, pre-
dicting the terrible fate which was to befall the city of Sidon,
declares as God's mouthpiece 'I will send pestilence in her
[midst] and bloodshed in her streets.' There follows, in the
massoretic Hebrew text, the expression וְנִפְלַל חָלָל בְּחוּצוֹתֶיהָ
which can only mean 'and the slain [or wounded, lit. the
pierced one] shall *be judged* in her midst.' Even if one were to
stretch the meaning of the doubtful word וְנִפְלַל in this context to imply 'the effect of being judged' and so 'to suffer
punishment', the continuity of thought required by the verse
would not satisfactorily be met. What is required is the detail-
ing of some calamity in keeping with the following words 'by
the sword against her all around'. The solution is furnished
by the *LXX* rendering πεσοῦνται 'shall fall', representing the
Hebrew וְנָפַל and by the Targum יִתְרְמְיוֹן 'shall be cast down'
which presupposes the same Hebrew word. Here we can see
that the final letter ל was accidentally duplicated by the copyist. The medieval commentator Kimhi, while correctly under-

standing the sense, suggests that this duplication is, in fact, a rare grammatical verbal form of the root נפל. However, by restoring the normal verbal form the text runs smoothly as 'the slain [or wounded] shall fall in her midst by the sword against her all around.'

Now an example of a whole word accidentally repeated by the copyist: Our reference is Psalm 45: 5, the first word of which is suspect. Taking the end of verse 4 and the beginning of verse 5 together we find them to be וַהֲדָרֶךָ (v. 5): הוֹדְךָ וַהֲדָרֶךָ (v. 4). In praising the virtues of the king the Psalmist exclaims, in verse 4 'Gird your sword upon [your] thigh. O mighty one; it is your glory and your majesty'. The first word in verse 5 is the same one ending verse 4, and the RSV, by retaining it, is forced to render, or rather to interpret it, to mean 'and *in* your majesty (ride forth...)'. Bearing in mind that the ancient manuscripts did not have any verse divisions, it is easy to see how the copyist, having written this word twice instead of once, made the reader consider the duplicated word as the beginning of the next verse. In the *LXX* (enumerated as Psalm 44: 4) the translators found this word at the beginning of verse 5, but they translated it ἔντεινον, that is as a verb in the imperative, meaning 'stretch', pointing to the word וְהִדְרֹךְ— 'and bend [the bow] '. As against the *LXX* rendering being influenced evidently by the reference in verse 4 to the king's girding on his sword, we note that, in verse 5 there is a change of theme, in that the Psalmist here speaks of the king's moral attributes, exhorting him 'ride on [the crest of] truth and rightdoing'. What is of incidental interest in the *LXX* rendering is that it provides evidence that, at the time that this translation was made, this dittograph was already established in the text and is therefore earlier than the date of translation.

An interesting example of dittography is found in the opening words of 1 Samuel 20: 3 וַיִּשָּׁבַע עוֹד דָּוִד 'David again [or further] took an oath and said ...'. There is nothing in the preceding verses to suggest that the oath taken by David was a supplementary one, so that one would suspect the word עוֹד

to be redundant. In fact, it is due to dittography. When we restore the continuous consonantal wording of the text we find that the reading before the copyist was וישבעדוד, which should have been divided into the two words וַיִּשָׁבַע דָוִד 'then David took an oath'. The copyist, however, repeated in writing the last letter of the first word and the first letter of the second word, making the combination עד and read as עוד. Incidentally the *LXX* rendering of the first word, ἀπεκρίθη represents the Hebrew וַיַּשֶׁב –'and [David] answered'.

It may come as a surprise to learn that, in some instances, a whole phrase, consisting of several words, was inadvertently repeated by a copyist. An interesting case of this larger dittography is seen in Joshua 4: 7. In this passage Joshua instructs the people how they were to answer questions which might be asked of them at some future time as to why large stones had been placed in the bed of the river Jordan. They were to explain that these stones commemorate the crossing of the Jordan by the invading Hebrew tribes under the leadership of Joshua. In the words of the massoretic text 'the waters of Jordan were cut off נִכְרְתוּ מֵימֵי הַיַּרְדֵּן before the ark of the covenant of the Lord when it crossed over the Jordan *the waters of the Jordan were cut off* (נִכְרְתוּ מֵי הַיַּרְדֵּן). It is obvious that the second reference to the cutting off of the waters of the Jordan is a dittography from the line above, the copyist's eye having wandered back to the beginning of the line after he had copied the whole line. This is quite a natural kind of miscopying.

The same kind of dittography, but in this case of a whole verse and the beginning of the next one, occurs in the Qumran scroll in Isaiah 38: 20. The preceding verse (19) reads in the massoretic text חַי חַי הוּא יוֹדֶךָ כָּמוֹנִי הַיוֹם אָב לְבָנִים יוֹדִיעַ אֶל אֲמִתֶּךָ –'the living, the living thank [or confess to] thee as I [do] this day, as a father makes thy truth known, O God, to his sons.' Incidentally, we read אֵל ('God') for the massoretic אֶל ('to'), as will soon be explained. Verse 20 opens with the words יהוה לְהוֹשִׁיעֵנִי –'the Lord will save me'. In the Qumran text all this is faithfully reproduced, but it is followed by a repetition of the entire verse 19 and the two opening words of verse 20. What happened seems to have been as follows. The two opening words of verse 20 were evidently at the end of the line in the manuscript the copyist at Qumran had before him, following upon the whole of verse 19 in that line. It seems that, having completed writing this line, his eye wandered back to the beginning of this line, with the result that he repeated the whole line, that is verse 19 and the first two words of verse 20. While one would not be dogmatic in offering this explanation, it nevertheless does explain this remarkable dittography of more than an entire verse. It is to be noted also that, in the repeated line, the copyist wrote the word אלוה ('God') before אמתך, thereby clearly indicating that the word אל in verse 19 was read as אֵל ('God') and not אֶל ('to').

An example of a partial dittography may be seen in 2 Samuel 13: 33. In the preceding verse is the statement that 'Amnon alone was dead'—כִּי אַמְנוֹן לְבַדּוֹ מֵת—but it is repeated in verse 33 as כִּי אִם אַמְנוֹן with the massoretic note that אם was not to be read—a clear case of dittography. It is to be noted that the final forms of letters are a late introduction, so that our present writing of אם would have been אמם.

Not all cases of dittography are as straightforward as these. We have given here an example of a partial dittography corrected by the Rabbis, but sometimes a word which is only partially repeated may result in the corruption of that word. This kind of partial dittography is well illustrated by a comparison of the duplicated texts in 2 Kings 19: 23 and Isaiah 37: 24. We are here dealing with the same text, as it appears in two different books. In this passage the prophet Isaiah castigates Sannacherib, king of Assyria, for his arrogant boasting in declaring 'with the multitude of my chariots I ascended the heights of the mountains'. In the Isaiah text the opening words of this verse are correctly בְּרֹב רִכְבִּי but, in the corresponding text in 2 Kings, we find the curious ברכב רכבי. The first word in the latter reading is emended by the Massoretes to conform to the correct reading of the Isaiah text. To explain how the corruption was introduced into the 2 Kings text, we would say that the copyist wrote down the first two letters of the word ברב, namely בר, and then his eye wandered to the next word which began with the letter ר and completed the word by copying in the second one, thereby producing the hybrid form ברכב. He nevertheless continued writing the next word, as if it had not at all influenced his miscopying of the preceding one.

We might note, in passing, a slight discrepancy in the wording of the opening words of this verse in each of the two parallel texts. In 2 Kings 19: 23 the phrase used is בְּיַד מַלְאָכֶיךָ—'by your messengers'—whereas in Isaiah 37: 24 we find בְּיַד עֲבָדֶיךָ—'by your servants'.[3] While it is necessary to note such discrepant traditional readings, the fact that there is no difference in the sense does not pose any textual problem and either reading is acceptable. This is an example of how discrepant textual readings are to be found in duplicated passages and, in our example, it is sufficient to record that such variants in wording, though not in the sense, somehow came about. An example of a variant reading in the Qumran text of Isaiah 31: 5 with the same meaning as the word in the massoretic text is והפליט for והמליט, both in the sense of 'he rescues'.

E. *Haplography: the failure on the part of the copyist to repeat a letter, a group of letters in a word, or even a whole word*

In the Babylonian talmudic tractate Nedarim 37b-38a a list is given of haplographies which the Rabbis recognized in the Hebrew Bible. These, by no means complete, are given under the heading הלין קריין ולא כתיבן—'these [words] are to be read [i.e. supplied by the reader] though they are not written [in the biblical text]'. Our first example comes from Judges 20: 13. In the printed editions of the Hebrew Bible we find the

---

[3] The *LXX* had ἀγγέλων in both texts, representing the reading מַלְאָכֶיךָ

curious line וְלֹא אָבוּ .. בְּנְיָמִן. The empty space indicates a missing word with the vowel-points of that word. The massoretic directive here is בני קרי ולא כתיב, that is, 'you must [supply the] read[ing] בְּנֵי which is not [in the] written [text]'. We can see how the copyist made his mistake when we restore that consonantal text, which was בניבנימין. It is clear that the copyist copied only one combination of בני instead of two. The massoretically restored line reads intelligibly 'the sons of Benjamin were not willing to listen'.

We turn to the Qumran Isaiah scroll for a similar example of haplography. The end of 26: 3 and the beginning of verse 4 are, in the massoretic text, כִּי בְךָ בָטוּחַ: בִּטְחוּ ביהוה—'For in thee there is trust. Trust ye in the Lord . . .' In the Qumran text, however, the last word of verse 3 is missing. In the consonantal early manuscripts with no verse division the text ran thus: בטחבטח. It is clear that a copyist of the Qumran recension wrote the word once instead of twice.

A haplography of a single letter in the massoretic text of Isaiah 23: 2 might be indicated by the corresponding reading in the Qumran text. The massoretic reading is (with reference to the merchants of Sidon) 'passing over the sea they have replenished you' (מִלְאוּךְ, in the ancient text was written מלאכ). The Qumran text reads מלאכיך 'your messengers [pass over the sea]', to which we should attach the beginning of verse 3 'in many waters'. The Qumran reading is certainly appropriate, while the massoretic text is not. It seems, then, that the text originally read מלאכך and the copyist of the massoretic recension wrote the כ only once instead of twice. Likewise in 40: 12 the masssoretic text reads 'who have measured the waters (מַיִם) in the hollow of his hand and marked the heavens with a span?' The Qumran text read מי ים 'the waters of the sea' for the massoretic מים, and seems more appropriate to the second half of the line. We conclude that the original text had the reading מיים and that the copyist of the massoretic text wrote the letter י only once instead of twice.

To see that the tendency to haplography was not an unusual feature of the work of the biblical copyist we have only to refer to the first chapter of Isaiah verse 2, where the word וַהֲרוֹמַמְתִּי ('and I have raised up') in the massoretic text appears as ורומתי in the Qumran text. The copyist wrote the letter מ once instead of twice and the missing letter was supplied, most likely by another hand, over the word. Similarly the word בִּעֲתַתְנִי 'terrified me' in 21: 4 appears in the Qumran text as בעתני, with missing letter above.

2 Samuel 18: 20 provides an example of the omission of a word by haplography due to its close resemblance to a following word. In the printed Hebrew edition the received text reads כִּי עַל ‥ בֶּן־הַמֶּלֶךְ מֵת indicating, as in the earlier example, that a word is missing and the Massoretes supplied the vowel-sound it had under the empty space. The Massoretes rightly direct that the word כֵּ be restored in reading before the word בֶּן. The line now reads smoothly 'because the king's son is dead'. The word כן was overlooked by the copyist because of its close resemblance to the following word בן.

A parallel example of this kind of haplography is found in Genesis 47: 16. In this chapter we are told that during the years of famine in Egypt the official controller of food stocks, Joseph, had sold corn to the people for money. When, however, their money was exhausted, they approached Joseph with the simple request הָבָה לָּנוּ לֶחֶם 'give us bread' (v. 15). Joseph replied 'give [me] your cattle and I will give you (וְאֶתְּנָה לָכֶם) for your cattle'. This line is defective, in that it does not state what Joseph offered them in exchange for their cattle. The *LXX* supplies the missing word, for it rendered this line as 'I will give you *bread* (ἄρτους) for your cattle'. The missing word in the Hebrew text is לֶחֶם; its omission in the massoretic text was due to its close resemblance, both in writing and in sound, to the following word לָכֶם. Thus we are entitled to restore the missing word and, if it is felt that additional confirmation is needed, we have only to look at the following verse (17) in this passage. Here we find the information that 'they brought their cattle to Joseph and he gave them *bread* . . .' The tendency to omit a letter in a word because it looked like the following one is illustrated also in the Qumran Isaiah scroll 4: 1, where we find the word וְהֶחֱזִיקוּ written והחֱזיקה; the ח was accidentally omitted because of its close resemblance to the preceding letter ה. In the ancient script these letters are ג and ห.

We now cite an example of a haplography due to the very close similarity of two words being immediately together in the line but, in this instance, the resemblance is seen in the ancient Hebrew script and not in the familiar square script. The last part of 1 Samuel 9: 16 reads כִּי רָאִיתִי אֶת־עַמִּי which literally means 'for I [God] have seen my people' and this is followed by the assurance that 'his cry has reached me'. The sense which the Hebrew words could suggest, if taken to be normal language, would be 'I have taken note of [i.e. will do something for] my people', but this interpretation is not satisfactory. The *LXX* rendering is ἐπέβλεψα ἐπὶ τὴν ταπείνωσιν τοῦ λαοῦ μου 'I have looked upon the low state of my people' and the Targum reads גְּלֵי קֳדָמַי דּוּחֲקָא דְעַמִּי 'the distress of my people is revealed before me'. Both versions imply a Hebrew text which read רָאִיתִי אֶת־עֱנִי עַמִּי 'I have seen *the distress of* my people' and this fits in perfectly with what follows. When we rewrite the last two words in the archaic script we have ꀔ. It thus becomes immediately clear that the copyist overlooked the first word because of its close resemblance to the one immediately following it. He might even have thought that he had before him a case of dittography which required correction. This example shows that when the textual critic is faced with a problem in the Hebrew text which is not amenable to solution on the basis of the familiar script, he will write out the line in the ancient script and this reconstruction might point to the answer.

In Jeremiah 31: 37[4] a similar haplographic omission by a copyist, due to the juxtaposition of two words of closely

---

[4] v. 38 in Kittel's Biblia Hebraica.

similar appearance, was noted and corrected by the Massoretes. In the printed Hebrew Bible the defective line is הִנֵּה יָמִים ‪ ‬ ‪.‬ נְאֻם יהוה 'Behold, days . . . . . said the Lord'. The word missing in this oft-repeated prophetic-introductory formula (as in vv. 26 and 30 in this chapter[5]) is בָּאִים 'are coming'. Once again, in order to understand how the omission of this word came about we rewrite the two words as they had been in the early consonantal succession of letters, namely באמנאם. Seen in this form we can readily understand how the copyist overlooked the word באם, because it looked very much like the following one נאם. In the ancient Hebrew script the writing would have been ᔎ𐤀ᔎᔎ𐤀ᔎ .

F. *Homoioteleuton*

This type of error is due to the following. When a word in a line, or a phrase, is repeated in the next line and the copyist has written the word in the first line, his eye wanders to this word in the next line and continues from there. He thus omits all the words inbetween. The massoretic text of 1 Samuel 13: 15 illustrates this phenomenon well. It reads: 'Then Samuel arose and he went up from *Gilgal* to Gibea of Benjamin.' The *LXX* read: 'Then Samuel arose and departed from *Gilgal* and the remnant of the people went after Saul to meet the warriors when they had come out of *Gilgal* to Gibea of Benjamin.' When we translate the Greek back into Hebrew it reads: וַיָּקָם שְׁמוּאֵל וַיַּעַל מִן הַגִּלְגָּל וְיֶתֶר הָעָם עָלָה אַחֲרֵי שָׁאוּל לִקְרֵאת עַם־הַמִּלְחָמָה בְּבֹאָם מִן־הַגִּלְגָּל גִּבְעַת בִּנְיָמִן We thus see that the copyist of the massoretic text, having written הַגִּלְגָּל in the first line continued from that word in the next line, thus omitting a whole line between.

The copyist of the Qumran text of Isaiah committed a similar error of homoioteleuton in Chapter 4: 5. It reads, in translation: 'Then the Lord will create over the whole site of Mount Zion and over her assemblies a cloud by day (יוֹמָם) and smoke and the shining of a flaming fire by night; for over all the glory

___
[5] vv. 27 and 31 in Kittel's Biblia Hebraica.

will be a canopy [v. 5] and a pavilion as a shade by day (יוֹמָם) from the heat.' In the Isaiah scroll of Qumran verse 5 ends with the first יומם and verse 6 begins with the word after the second יומם. Thus all the words between the two mentions of יומם were omitted by the copyist. Having written the first one, his eye wandered to the same word on the next line and he continued from there. As mentioned earlier, one of the great advantages of the Qumran biblical scrolls is that we have in them unmistakable examples of types of copyists' errors.

G. *Wrong vocalization of a correct consonantal text*

A good example of how the sense of a perfectly correct text may be distorted through misreading a consonantal word— that is, by providing the wrong vocalization—is seen in the *LXX* rendering of the end of Genesis 15: 11. In the earlier part of this chapter the narrator describes the preparations made by Abraham for the formal entering into a covenant relationship with God. He halved the three animals he had slaughtered and placed each piece opposite the corresponding half. When birds of prey swooped on the carcasses, Abraham drove them off—וַיַּשֵּׁב אֹתָם אַבְרָם. The *LXX* rendering is, strangely, συνεκάθισεν αὐτοῖς —'he sat down with them'. having obviously misread the consonantal words וישב אתם as וַיֵּשֶׁב אִתָּם. What is clear from this example is that the *LXX* translators had before them the same consonantal text as massoretic, but they misread and so misinterpreted the meaning of the two words.

Some scholars point to a misreading of a text in Proverbs 3: 25 which, in the masssoretic tradition, is אַל תִּירָא מִפַּחַד פִּתְאֹם —'Do not be afraid of sudden terror'. Since the second half of the verse reads 'or of the ruin of the wicked, when it comes', we can see that the first half does not balance the second. One would have expected the first half to have a noun corres- ponding to the word 'the wicked'. If, however, we vocalize the word (written consonantally פתאם) as פְּתָאִים 'the foolish', we have restored the balance between the two halves of the verse, since the author associates 'wickedness' with 'folly'.

H. *Errors in copying due to misinterpretation*

In the section dealing with the accidental transposition of letters within a word by a copyist it was explained that this was often due to his misunderstanding the text he was copying. The examples which follow illustrate in a general way how the distortion of a word can be made by a copyist through his misunderstanding of the context in which the word occurs. One such case is 1 Samuel 17: 7. In the preceding two verses a detailed description is given of the massive armour of the Philistine giant Goliath. Verse 7, continuing the catalogue of his weapons, should have begun with וְעֵץ חֲנִיתוֹ 'the wooden part of his spear [was like a weaver's beam]' as we find it in the duplicated passage of 2 Samuel 21: 19. Surprisingly, the text in 1 Samuel reads וְחֵץ חֲנִיתוֹ 'the arrow(s) of his spear', which makes no sense at all. The Massoretes restored the correct word by directing the reader to substitute the *K^erê* word וְעֵץ for the *K^etîb* וְחֵץ. It would seem that the copyist's mind was so concentrated on the details of Goliath's formidable armour that he misread this word as another item in this catalogue.

In Isaiah 10: 32 the prophet, speaking of the invader advancing towards Jerusalem, describes him as 'waving his hand [or, according to the NEB, giving the signal to advance] against הַר בֵּית צִיּוֹן [in the *K^etîb*] the mountain of the *house* of Zion'. This is corrected by the Massoretes to (the *K^erê*) הַר בַּת צִיּוֹן 'the mountain of the *daughter* of Zion'. The latter is the reading in the Qumran scroll of Isaiah. The target of the enemy's attack was the people of Jerusalem, designated as 'daughter of Zion', whereas the copyist thought the reference was to the Temple mount—'*the mount of the Temple of Zion*'.

A comparison between the duplicated texts of 2 Kings 20: 13 and Isaiah 39: 2 shows how, in the former, the copyist misunderstood the text he was transcribing. The king of Babylon sent an embassy to King Hezekiah of Judah with gifts, for he had heard that Hezekiah had been ill. The reaction of Hezekiah to this patronizing gesture is described in the text of 2 Kings as וַיִּשְׁמַע עֲלֵיהֶם 'he listened to them', implying that he showed subservience to these royal envoys. The Isaiah text, however, reads וַיִּשְׂמַח עֲלֵיהֶם meaning, literally, 'he rejoiced', i.e. 'he was delighted with them [JB]' or 'he made them welcome [NEB]'. Since he showed them round his palace and proudly displayed his treasures to them, we would see in Hezekiah's response that he was highly flattered, and delighted. The Isaiah reading is, therefore, most likely the correct reading which should have been in the text of 2 Kings. The copyist misunderstood the intent of the writer and, having written the letters וישמ of the word he finished it as וישמע. The *LXX* has the correct text in both passages.

A similar misinterpretation of what the writer intended to convey is seen by some scholars in Proverbs 3: 10. The verse, as it stands in the massoretic text, reads 'your barns will be full of *plenty* (שָׂבָע) and your vats will be bursting with wine'. The rules of parallelism in ancient Hebrew poetry suggest that, whereas the reference to 'vats' is balanced by that of 'barns', the notion of 'plenty' is too general a term to balance the mention of 'wine'. To make the parallelism true some specific food substance is required in the first half of the verse to correspond to the 'wine' in the vats. The *LXX* rendering σίτῳ 'with corn' is the exact parallel to '"wine' and, when we retranslate the Greek back into Hebrew, we have the word שֶׁבֶר. If this is the original word, it is easy to see how the copyist was misled in his reading of the text before him. He began writing the correct word but, having written the first two letters שב and, his mind being on the theme of plentiful food, he finished writing this word as שבע 'plenty'. The above examples indicate the need on the part of the textual critic when confronted with a clearly faulty text, to investigate the possibility of a misunderstanding by a copyist of what the writer intended. Often such misunderstandings are influenced by the correct word having the initial letters in common with another familiar word which the copyist thought, mistakenly, was in keeping with the context of the verse.

In the presentation of massoretic Hebrew grammar it should
be pointed out that many of the rules involving internal
changes in words are simply statements of what actually
happens in speech and of the tendency to represent such
changes by corresponding modifications in spelling. In speech
the weak letter א, most likely originally representing a glottal
stop, came to be merely the carrier of a vowel-sound and is
unheard. When it has a vowel-sound but is preceded by a
vowelless letter, it often cedes its vowel-sound to that letter:
e.g. an original רְאָשִׁים becoming רָאשִׁים ('heads'). There are
many instances in the text of the Hebrew Bible of an א being
omitted in the spelling, but where the missing א could give rise
to the possibility of the defectively written word being
wrongly identified with another word, the Massoretes usually
supply the note א׳ חָסֵר that is, 'an א is missing'. The following
are some examples of words written defectively, i.e. without
the א, to which the Massoretes drew attention. Genesis 25: 24,
תוֹמִם is to be read תְּאוֹמִים 'twins'; Numbers 11: 11, מָצָתִי to be
read מָצָאתִי 'I have found'; and 1 Samuel 1: 17, שֵׁלָתֵךְ to be
read שְׁאֵלָתֵךְ 'your request'. We might add a few examples from
the Qumran scroll of Isaiah, where the missing א is restored
above the word by a later reviser of the text. We reproduce
them as they appear in the scroll: 8: 23, הרישון for the massoretic
הָרִאשׁוֹן 'the first'; 36: 16, תנתו for תְּאֵנָתוֹ 'his fig tree'; and
41: 11, יובדו for יֹאבְדוּ 'they perish'.

The phenomenon of omitting the א in a word in writing to
correspond to its omission in articulation might solve a very
difficult reading in Job 5: 5. In the massoretic text this verse
consists of three parts, but, for the sake of simplicity we shall
consider only the first and third sections. (It is possible that
the medial line is a later insertion into the text of a note, designated as a gloss, a phenomenon with which we shall deal
later (p. 79 ff.). In Hebrew the two balancing lines read
אֲשֶׁר קְצִירוֹ רָעֵב יֹאכֵל... וְשָׁאַף צַמִּים חֵילָם   'whose harvest the hungry one will eat ... and the *snare* pants after their wealth'.
The elementary rule of parallelism in ancient Hebrew poetry

requires a word to correspond with 'the hungry'. Some minor Greek versions and the Syriac version render the enigmatic word צָמִים as 'the thirsty ones', that is צְמֵאִים, written defectively צמים and read צְמֵים. The theme of this line seems to be that the nomad will raid the farmer's field and the description of the nomad as 'the hungry one' is finely paralleled by the following epithet 'the thirsty one(s)'. One would, therefore, be inclined to see in this reading the restoration of the original word and it would explain the dilemma in the massoretic text as being due to the omission of the silent א by the copyist in his copying this word as, indeed, it was in the articulated word. Some critics suggest, furthermore, that the singular צָמֵא –'the thirsty one' was in the original text, balancing the singular רָעֵב –'the hungry one' in the first part of the verse and that the מ properly belongs to the next word as a prefixed preposition *'from* their wealth'.

There is evidence to show that in the course of time the letter ע had ceased to have its guttural sound and was not heard in the spoken word. We have only to turn to the Qumran scroll of Isaiah to see examples of the omission of this letter in words, evidently in keeping with the weakening of this letter virtually to that of an א. In this manuscript the missing letter ע is supplied over words, possibly by a correcting hand. In the opening line of Isaiah we find the name of the prophet written ישׁ^עיהו, that is, written as articulated—ישׁיהו and corrected to read ישׁעיהו; in 5: 21 בעיניהם, written by the copyist ביניהם, as it was evidently pronounced, is corrected to read בעיניהם 'in their eyes'; and in 9: 7 ביעקב which sounded בְּיַקֹב in speech, is restored to read ביעקב 'in Jacob'. Some scholars explain the Hebrew word בִּי 'please'—the normal polite way of introducing a statement—as a defective spelling for בְּעִי which they identify with the verbal root בָּעָה 'sought', 'requested', and which is the usual word in Aramaic in the form בְּעָא.

The loss of the guttural sound of the letter ע and the tendency shown by some copyists to write words phonetically

sometimes led to a misinterpretation of a verse. This tendency is most likely when, like the letter א, it has a vowel
sound but is preceded by a consonant which is vowelless;
the now-silent ע cedes its vowel-sound to the preceding letter. This kind of error is well exemplified in Amos 8: 8,
where the line should read '[the land] shall be tossed about
and shall *sink* (וְנִשְׁקְעָה) like the Nile of Egypt.' The copyist,
however, wrote the above Hebrew word as וְנִשְׁקָה. Because the
letter ע had become silent (like the letter א), the word וְנִשְׁקְעָה
was evidently articulated as וְנִשְׁקָה and copied as such. The
copyist may also have been influenced by the verb שׁקה which,
in the Hiphil (causative) verbal form means 'watered', 'irri-
gated', and since the reference in this verse was to the Nile,
he associated the word with the annual overflow of this great
river which had the effect of irrigating the surrounding fields.
In the printed Hebrew Bible the attention of the reader is
drawn to the error and its correction firstly by attaching the
vowel-points of the correct word to the consonants of the
erroneous one in the text, thereby producing the impossible
form וְנִשְׁקָה. The reader, then, turns to the footnote where he
finds the *K^e rê* correction to be read.

It is curious, however, that an unmistakable error in the
preceding part of the verse should have been left uncorrected.
It should have read 'and all of it shall rise like *the Nile*' (כַּיְאוֹר),
referring to the annual rise of this river. This Hebrew word
was miscopied as כָּאוֹר ('like the light'), which is clearly not in
line with the context. The implication here is that the weak
letter י was, likewise, not heard in the spoken word and that
the copyist wrote down this word as it was sounded. It is of
course possible that the scribe simply left out a letter and
read 'light' in anticipation of this word in the next verse. It is
rather surprising that the Rabbis did not correct this word,
particularly as this whole expression appears in its correct
form in chapter 9, verse 5. The Aramaic Targum, however,
did have the correct sense, for it rendered it כְּמֵי נַהֲרָא –'like the
waters of the river'. Both Rashi and Kimhi point out the
omission of the letter י.

That in some instances the letter ׳ had lost its consonantal character and became a silent letter is made clear from the following examples. The name of David's father Jesse is יִשַׁי in Hebrew and is found thus in 1 Chronicles 2 at the end of verse 12. At the beginning of verse 13, however, his name appears as אִישָׁי. Turning to the Qumran scroll of Isaiah, we find that the word for 'nations' is always spelled גּוֹיִם in the massoretic Hebrew text, but as גואים in the Qumran text. The fact that some copyists wrote words phonetically, omitting in spelling an א, ע, or even ׳, and that this practice sometimes led, in later times, to a misunderstanding of words, is of significance for the textual critic, since the scope of possible restorations is thereby enlarged.

The examples in this chapter will give the student some idea of the range of textual criticism within the area of recognized types of copyists' errors. As demonstrated in each example, some types of miscopying are to be found corrected in the massoretic lists, while other instances of the same types of error have been identified and corrected by reference to duplicated passages in the Hebrew Bible and to the ancient versions, as well as by the contexts of verses where no external aid is available. Our next task is to deal with errors which cannot be placed in definite categories and whose solutions are sought by sensible sober judgement.

(footnote to p. 70)

[1] This word is found in the parallel text 2 Kings 18:26. In the massoretic text of Isaiah the word is אֵלֵינוּ "to us." The Qumran text should have had this word after ואל תדבר "and do not speak (with us)." The word יְהוּדִית 'Judean' is not in the Qumran text, but it has the variant "these words."

5

UNSPECIFIED TYPES OF ERROR

UNDER this heading we firstly draw attention to several examples of mistakes in copying which can be explained only as being due to sheer carelessness or, possibly, fatigue. These include the leaving out of a letter in a word and thereby distorting it, and the overlooking of a whole word and even a whole line. Evidence of such careless copying in the complete Qumran text of Isaiah is seen in the clumsy mode of correcting such faults, evidently by a hand other than that of the copyist. Omitted letters are restored in the space above the faulty words and missing words are replaced either between the lines or, if a whole line had been omitted, it is restored in vertical sequence down the outside of the column. Such corrupted copying which, as we shall illustrate, occurs in the massoretic Hebrew text as well as the Qumran Isaiah text, is not attributable to any misunderstanding of the text or to any variant traditional readings but to human weakness.

In Isaiah 39: 8b the simple and familiar word וַיֹּאמֶר ('and he said') is found in the Qumran text in the form ויאמ. It is quite evident that the copyist failed to write in the last letter of this word and, because there was no space available between this word and the following one, the missing letter was restored above the end of the defective word. In 20: 2 the word הַשָּׂק ('the sackcloth') was not copied in at all and, again, because there was no space in the line for its insertion, it was written in the space above between the preceding and following words. In 36: 11 the copyist overlooked the word עִמָּנוּ[1]('with us') and, in this instance, the restoration was made by its insertion at the beginning of the line, but outside the column. In chapter 5 verse 8 the massoretic text reads 'and you shall be made [NEB left] to dwell—וְהוּשַׁבְתֶּם —alone in the land". The *LXX* rendering οἰκήσετε presupposes the Kal (simple active) reading וִישַׁבְתֶּם 'and you shall dwell'. This, in fact, was the reading in the Qumran text, but the copyist wrote וישתם, leaving out the letter ב. Strangely, the missing letter was not restored above the word over the place where it should have been written. Evidently, this careless mistake was not noticed by the reviser of the text.

In 11: 4 the Qumran reading is 'by the breath of his [God's] lips [i.e. by his word] the wicked shall be put to death'— יומת רשע—for the massoretic יָמִית רָשָׁע 'he shall slay the wicked'. We are not concerned here with these two divergent readings in the massoretic and the Qumran recensions as shown by the supplying of different vowel letters to the consonantal word ימת. The reader of the Qumran text will be surprised to find that the copyist wrote these two words *before* the expression 'by the breath of his lips' and then wrote them again after them where they properly belong. To erase this misplaced writing, dots were placed over and below the first insertion of these words to draw the attention of the reader to this muddle and to indicate that they were to be ignored. A different mode of erasion was used in the Qumran text of Isaiah 21: 1, where the expression מֵאֶרֶץ נוֹרָאָה 'from a terrible land' is found as מארץ רחֹוקֳה ‏ נראה. The offending word was eliminated by a stroke placed through it and the established word over it. While, on the one hand, it is possible that the copyist's mind wandered from the text before him and he wrote in the familiar phrase 'from a distant land', which had threatening overtones, it is also likely that the erased word could have represented a variant traditional reading which was emended to conform to the standard text.

In the massoretic Hebrew Bible there is no lack of examples of faulty copying which can only be explained in terms of carelessness or, as suggested earlier, through fatigue. One such instance may be seen in Isaiah 20: 5. The unpointed Qumran text reads 'they shall be dismayed and ashamed at Cush their *trust—* מבטחם (מִבְטָחָם)—and at Egypt their glory'. The *LXX* and the Targum agree with this reading which seems to be correct, since the two nouns balance each other well. The massoretic text, however, reads מַבָּטָם. The plain meaning of this noun is ['the object of] their gaze', so that we would have to say that its sense was extended by interpretation to mean 'their hope'. Since the verbal form הִבִּיט (in the causative Hiphil), meaning 'looked (at)', is often used in contexts implying 'sympathy', 'caring for', the nominal form could possibly be made to fit the sense required by the line. However, in the light of the Qumran reading, supported by the *LXX* and the Targum, coupled with the fact that its sense is direct and not implied, we are led to the conclusion that the copyist of the massoretic text carelessly omitted the letter ח in this word and wrote מבטם instead of מבטחם.

The above examples of faulty copying in the Qumran text of Isaiah are clearly illustrated and not inferred; they point to errors which cannot be grouped under any of the headings treated in Chapter 4. Though the explanation of careless copying widens the scope of textual criticism, extreme restraint must be exercised by the critic, for otherwise an uncontrollable spate of emendations could be unleashed in attempts to rectify the errors. Where a case of miscopying is established and no aid is forthcoming from the ancient versions or from parallel texts, and the miscopying cannot be identified with a particular type of error, then the context will be the main factor in determining what was the most likely original reading.

We now turn to an examination of some duplicated passages in the Hebrew Bible, where discrepancies in readings cannot be accounted for in terms of types of scribal errors. We shall see that these divergencies in readings reveal a large variety of possibilities in human fallibility in the copying of manuscripts. We refer firstly to the Song of David, as it appears in 2 Samuel: 22 and again in Psalm 18. While some discrepancies might easily be explained and others do not affect the sense of the line, there are situations in which the

ingenuity of the textual critic is taxed and he might find himself in the unsatisfactory state of not being able to go beyond
noting the difficulty posed by the discrepant readings in the
two recensions.

Verse 28 provides an excellent illustration of this kind of
dilemma. The first half of the verse reads 'thou [God] dost
deliver a lowly people'; this is straightforward and does not
present any difficulty. In the Psalms version this statement is
balanced by the second half of the verse which reads, in contrast, 'but proud eyes thou dost bring low' וְעֵינַיִם רָמוֹת תַּשְׁפִּיל.
The text in 2 Samuel, however, has the following discrepant
reading: וְעֵינֶיךָ עַל־רָמִים תַּשְׁפִּיל which can be taken to mean
either 'thou dost bring thine eyes low upon the haughty' or
'thine eyes [are] upon the haughty, thou dost bring [them]
low', This latter interpretation was adopted by the RSV, while
the NEB took this line to mean 'thou lookest with contempt
upon the haughty'. The JB, however, renders it as if the
Hebrew text in 2 Samuel were the same as the one in the
Psalms text, thereby showing preference for the Psalms reading. If we look to the rules of parallelism, we see that, though
the Psalms reading may require some adjustment, it points to
the correct sense, for it provides a contrasting balance in
thought between the two halves of the verse. This consideration might have influenced the translators of the JB to adopt
it as the original correct wording in the 2 Samuel text. One is
left with the firm impression that something went wrong in
the transcription of this second half of the verse not only in
the 2 Samuel text but also in the Psalm version. The Psalms
reading is not faultless for, in strict conformity with the rules
of parallelism, we would have expected the second half of the
verse to be 'but the eyes of *the haughty one* [in the singular]
thou dost bring low': וְעֵינֵי רָם תַּשְׁפִּיל. The rule of parallelism in
Hebrew poetry suggests that the medial word רָם 'the haughty
one' was, most likely, the original reading corresponding, by
contrast, with עָנִי 'the lowly one'. We are now faced with the
option of either doing nothing more than stating the facts of

the situation or, alternatively, hazarding some kind of explanation to account for these incongruities. From the consonantal text even in the square script there is some indication
of what might have gone wrong in transcription if we hold
the view that, in some early manuscripts, the words were
written in continuous lettering without strict word divisions.
Looking at the text as emended before, namely ועינירמתתשפל,
it is possible that, in the Psalms text, there is a dittography of
the letter ת. Having, then, written this word as רמת (pointed
as רָמוֹת, a feminine-plural adjective), the copyist had to emend
the construct form וְעֵינֵי –'and the eyes of'–to the absolute
form וְעֵינַיִם or perhaps he considered the former as an abbre-
viated form of the latter. Turning, now, to the copyist of the
2 Samuel text, it is possible that he transcribed the text before
him by confused dittography, reading the ר as כר and producing ועיניכר– וְעֵינֶיךָ 'and thine eyes'. He then had to introduce
the preposition עַל 'upon' to give his transcription some sense,
while he further indulged in the dittography of the letter מ,
writing רממ, (רָמִים 'the haughty ones'). The *LXX* (v. 27) rendering in both texts is the plural 'the haughty ones', though
different words are used in each case. This reconstruction of
what might have taken place, possibly by a succession of
copyists' errors, is presented as purely tentative. The reason
for this brief exercise is to demonstrate the kind of reasoning
which, theoretically, could be offered to account for the
unsatisfactory reading in the 2 Samuel text and, also, for
the slight correction thought to be necessary in the Psalms
text.

We note, incidentally, another discrepancy between the
opening words of this verse in the two recensions. The Samuel
text reads וְאֶת־עָם, while the parallel words in the Psalms are
כִּי אַתָּה עַם. Though there is no real difference in the sense, it
is worth pointing out, for reference in other texts where a
change in meaning might be involved, that what happened
was apparently as follows. In the archaic Hebrew script the
first letter of the first word was read as Ύ (ו) in the Samuel

text and as ־ֽי (כ) in the Psalms text. In the former it was
attached as a conjunctive to the next word and, in the latter,
it was read as a separate word and supplied with the appropriate vowel-letter—כִּי 'but'. The second word את was read as
אֵת, the sign of the definite object, in the 2 Samuel text and
as the personal pronoun אַתָּה 'thou' in the other text. While
reflecting different readings, they nevertheless bear testimony
to the same text as it was in the consonantal form without
vowel-letters.

A seemingly intractable problem is presented in the duplicated texts of verse 13 in 2 Samuel 22 and Psalm 18. The
former reads מִנֹּגַהּ נֶגְדּוֹ בָּעֲרוּ גַחֲלֵי אֵשׁ 'out of the brightness before him [God] coals of fire flamed'. The latter text has the
longer reading מִנֹּגַהּ נֶגְדּוֹ עָבָיו עָבְרוּ בָּרָד וְגַחֲלֵי אֵשׁ 'out of the
brightness before him [God] his thick clouds passed away;
hailstones and coals for fire'. How can one deal with two such
discrepant versions of the same text? In the first place we note
that the opening and closing words in both texts are the same
and, on that account, are to be regarded as likely original and
correct readings. Our problem is confined to the discrepancies in the middle of this verse. In the attempt to resolve this
problem all one can do is to suggest the kind of reasoning a
textual critic might apply in the endeavour to arrive at some
sensible explanation. He might argue that the expression 'his
thick clouds passed away' is appropriate to the context, since
the effect of the 'brightness before him' was that it dispelled
the thick clouds. How, then, did the copyist of the 2 Samuel
text come to omit them? Let us look at the writing in the
sequence of letters without vowel-letters as it could have
been in early manuscripts, namely עבועברבר . Did this look to
him like an unintelligible jumble of letters? עבועבר could
certainly suggest a dittography as, indeed, the two other
groups ברבר of the fifth and sixth and the seventh and eighth
letters. What about the variant readings בָּרָד 'hailstones' and
בָּעֲרוּ 'burned'? Is it possible that the text originally had the
combination ברו and that this was taken by the one inter-

pretation of the context to be defective for וֹ בָרָד and by the
other to be defective for בָּעֲרוּ bearing in mind that the letter
ע had, at some stage, ceased to have its guttural sound and
became silent, as demonstrated in Chapter 4, p. 67 above?
One might agree with those critics who argue that, if a noun
is to be read in this defectively written word, it should be בָּרָק
'lightning', which is described poetically as 'flaming coals'.
Critics will differ in their reconstruction of the original text,
as evidenced by the translations in the NEB and the JB. Perhaps the discussion should be left here, without our deciding
in favour of the one solution offered as against the other.
What is to be noted, however, is the interesting fact that in
the *LXX* (enumerated as verse 12) the variant massoretic
readings of 2 Samuel and of Psalm 18 (enumerated as 17) are
represented, thus testifying to the antiquity of this discrepancy. Before leaving this discussion we have to note further
that the following verse (14) reads 'The Lord thundered in the
heavens; the Most High gave forth his voice'. The Psalms
massoretic text has the additional 'hailstones and coals of fire
—a line obviously recopied accidentally from the preceding
verse. This is conclusively proved not only by its absence from
the text of 2 Samuel but also from the *LXX* rendering of the
Psalms text (v. 13). The two versions of the Song of David
exhibit many more discrepancies in readings, but we feel that
the two examples given above will suffice to demonstrate the
phenomenon of the mishandling of texts by the copyists. We
reserve a third example for the next chapter, for this involves
the incorporation of a gloss (pp. 81–83).

We now turn to Psalm 59 where we find two versions of
the same verse. The Psalm ends with the refrain עֻזִּי אֵלֶיךָ אֲזַמֵּרָה
כִּי אֱלֹהִים מִשְׂגַּבִּי אֱלֹהֵי חַסְדִּי 'O my strength, I will sing praises to
Thee, for God is my fortress, my God of steadfast love.' The
translators of the NEB omit the last phrase, no doubt regarding it as a pious gloss accidentally incorporated in the text—a
phenomenon which will be discussed later in Chapter 6.
Whether this is so or not, we have to consider it as part of the

verse which has come down to us and which, in fact, was in
the Hebrew text before the *LXX* translators. This refrain
occurs also in verse 10, dividing the Psalm into two parts, but
with some variations. It opens with the words עֻזּוֹ אֵלֶיךָ אֶשְׁמֹרָה
which, when taken literally, means '*his* strength, to thee *do I
watch*'. The *LXX* (58: 9) has the rendering of עֻזִּי, as at the
conclusion of the Psalm, which is what we would expect. It
seems, then, that in verse 10, the wrong possesive suffix had
been given to this noun. The word אֶשְׁמֹרָה was certainly in
the Hebrew text before the *LXX* translators, for they rendered 'I will keep my strength'. The NEB retains this reading in its translation 'to thee I turn in the night watches',
probably following the comment of Ibn Ezra that the reference
is to לֵיל שִׁמּוּרִים 'a night of watching [or guarding]'. Rashi,
however, understands this word to mean 'waiting' or 'hoping'
for God's help and this interpretation would seem to be a
possible expression of the basic meaning of this word. Whichever reading is the original, this example of discrepancy illustrates how a simple word can be read quite differently by
two interpreters. We note finally that the ending of the refrain
in verse 18, אֱלֹהֵי חַסְדִּי, whether original or an incorporated
note, does not end verse 10 but opens verse 11. Here we
have another example of the wrong division of verses. Without it, verse 11 reads, in perfect balance, 'God will [come to]
meet me; he will let me gaze [in triumph] at my enemies'.

Isaiah 9: 16 provides another example of miscopying which
does not look like a misinterpretation of the prophet's words
but was due to sheer negligence, the copyist's mind having
wandered away from the text before him. In the massoretic
text the verse reads: 'Therefore the Lord will not *rejoice*—
לֹא יִשְׂמָח—*over* their young men and will not have pity—
לֹא יְרַחֵם —on their orphans and widows'. Clearly the thought
'rejoice' is out of balance with the concept 'pity'. The Qumran
text, however, has the correct reading לאו יחמול 'he will not
have mercy', which exactly corresponds to the following
phrase. If the copyist was at all familiar with the basic rules

of parallelism in ancient Hebrew poetry, he should have realized that what he wrote infringes upon them. It looks as if
his mistake was simply a careless one, his mind having wandered from the context of the line. Curiously, the *LXX* (v. 17)
had the massoretic mistake in the text and this again testifies
to the antiquity of such careless miscopying being established
in the text. Again in Isaiah 21: 8 the massoretic Hebrew text
reads 'The lion cried out—וַיִּקְרָא אַרְיֵה—upon the watchtower,
O Lord, I stand continuously by day'. The lion crying out is
sheer nonsense and the attempt to understand it to mean 'as
a lion' is not only unwarranted but unhelpful. The Qumran
text has the correct word הרואה, meaning literally 'the one
seeing' and refers to the soldier on the lookout tower on the
city wall. Once again, the *LXX* had our massoretic reading,
but it took it to be the proper name אוּרִיָה 'Uriah' which, again,
yields no sense. This miscopying in the massoretic text cannot be attributed to any of the types of copyists' errors dealt
with in the preceding chapter. One can only conclude that it
was due either to sheer carelessness or to fatigue at the end of
a session of copying.

6

GLOSSES AND EDITORIAL NOTES

A GLOSS may be defined as the intrusion of an extraneous word or words into a text, thereby causing a dislocation in the thought sequence of the line. By disregarding the disturbing element in the line the smooth reading is restored. It seems that in ancient times, before the advent of separate commentaries on the text of the Hebrew Bible, it was customary to have official notes written above selected words in a text, when it was thought necessary to provide some elucidation of the intent of the writer or to supply some item of information. These expository notes are always brief, sometimes consisting only of single words, and were written, apparently, in manuscripts used for study and teaching. The fact that glosses are recognized by their being disturbing elements in texts indicates that these notes were orginally external to the texts they expounded and were obviously meant to remain so. In the course of time, however, they became incorporated into the body of texts and the differentiation between what was the original writing and what was an expository note was lost. Editorial notes, like glosses, are also expository in character, but they differ from them in that they do not cause any dislocation in the text and seem therefore to have been deliberately attached to it. This phenomenon will be the subject of the second part of this chapter. We turn now to an examination of glosses which, according to the information they provide, may be classified as (*a*) explanatory or exegetical, (*b*) variant traditional readings, and (*c*) pious sentiments.

(*a*) A simple example of an explanatory gloss is found in Joshua 1: 15. In this narrative Joshua addresses the tribes of Reuben, Gad, and half of Manasseh, reminding them of the solemn promise they had made to Moses. This was that they would join the rest of the tribes in the battles for the conquest

of Canaan and, when they had fulfilled their military obliga-
tions, they would be free to rejoin their families whom they
had left on the eastern side of the river Jordan and take possession of the territory allotted to them there by Moses. The
second half of verse 15 reads, in the massoretic text, 'then you
may return to your [allocated] land for possession *and you
shall take possession of it—*וִירִשְׁתֶּם אֹתָהּ—which Moses, the servant of the Lord gave you east of the Jordan'. The statement
'and you shall take possession of it' breaks the continuity in
the sequence of thought. Without it the line reads smoothly
'then you may return to your land . . . which Moses gave you
. . . ' . We explain the insertion of the two Hebrew words as
an explanatory note which informs the reader that by his
reference to the tribes *returning* to their allocated lands the
writer meant that they would formally or legally take up
possession of them. That we here have a gloss is to be inferred
from the fact that the expression breaks the continuity of the
line and this conclusion is confirmed by the fact that it does
not appear in the *LXX* version. This latter fact proves that
this interpolated note was not in the Hebrew text which lay
before the *LXX* translators. The observation might be made
that such an explanatory note was quite unnecessary, since
the purpose of their returning to their allotted lands should
have been clear to any literate reader. It is of interest to note,
however, that a characteristic feature of later rabbinic exposition is that it usually made explicit what, to an intelligent
reader, was clearly implied in a biblical text. We would say,
then, that the glossator, as represented in explanatory glosses
incorporated in the Hebrew text, set a pattern which was to
be followed by later generations of authorized biblical expositors. We finally draw attention to the omission of this intervening phrase in the translations of JB and NEB; this omission
points to the recognition by their respective translators of the
presence of a gloss in this text.

We now examine an explanatory gloss designed to extend
the information given by the writer and we refer to the dupli-

cate texts in Psalms 14 and 53. We are concerned here with
the opening words of verse 5 in the former Psalm which are
duplicated in verse 6 in the latter. In both Psalms there is the
line 'there they were struck with a great fear', but this statement is followed in Psalm 53 with the additional information
that לֹא הָיָה פָחַד. The plain meaning of these words is 'there was
no [reason for] fear', though the medieval Jewish commentator
Ibn Ezra interpreted them to mean 'there was never a dread
like it'. Whatever the true sense of the line is, the accretion in
Psalm 53 looks like an interpolated exegetical note, that is a
gloss. Not only is it not in the text of Psalm 14, but it inter-
rupts the flow of thought in the verse. The information it
purports to give was evidently meant to heighten the dramatic
effect of the poet's words when he speaks of the terrible fear
which gripped the evildoers. Curiously the *LXX* version in-
cludes this interposed comment in both Psalms (enumerated
as 13 and 52). This fact points to the antiquity of the practice
of writing in standard notes on selected lines and also of the
incorporation of such notes into the text by copyists. In both
instances this note had been firmly fixed in the Hebrew text
which the *LXX* translators had before them. We finally look
at the modern English versions of Psalm 53 because they
reflect the views of three different panels of scholars and
remind the student that unanimity among scholars is not
always achieved. The NEB omits this interposed comment
and thus regards it as an accretion. The JB and RSV, however,
retain it. The former, in translating it 'in terror such as had
not been' follows the interpretation of Ibn Ezra mentioned
above, while the latter's translation 'fear without reason'
adheres rather to the plain sense of the words.

We now consider an explanatory gloss with a different
interest. In the version of the Song of David in Psalm 18, verse
7, the note which was later incorporated in the text had evidently been designed to prevent the reader from taking the
poet's portrayal of God's response to prayer literally and in
anthropomorphic terms, that is to say, by assigning human

attributes to God. There is an additional value in comparing
the Psalms version with that of 2 Samuel 22, for it provides
an excellent example of the legitimate restoration of a defective
Hebrew text in which the distortion by the copyist is plain
for all to see. The second half of verse 7 in 2 Samuel 22 reads
'from his [God's] temple he heard my voice and my cry [was]
in his ears'—וְשַׁוְעָתִי בְּאָזְנָיו. The corresponding verse in the
Psalms text has 'from his temple he will hear my voice and
my cry before him shall come into his ears' —וְשַׁוְעָתִי לְפָנָיו תָּבֹא
בְּאָזְנָיו. Clearly something went wrong in both versions, since
one would have expected the number of words in the second
stanza to be neither two nor four but three, following the
pattern of this part of the poem. We have to account, then,
for the loss of one word in the 2 Samuel text and the accretion of an extra word in the Psalms text. Looking firstly at
the 2 Samuel text, we ask ourselves which of the two intervening words of the Psalms text is appropriate to the word
בְּאָזְנָיו 'in his ears'. There will be no difficulty in deciding that
it is the verb תָּבֹא 'shall come' and this is missing from the 2
Samuel text. We have now to account for its omission by the
copyist of 2 Samuel. When we write out this part of the verse
in its original consonantal form of seemingly continuous letters without vowel-letters or word divisions we can see how
the copyist of the 2 Samuel text was faced with a dilemma.
When confronted with ושועתתבאבאזנו he must have concluded
that he had before him a set of two dittographies. He therefore copied the letter ת and the combination בא only once
each instead of twice.

This sample of a dual haplography is intelligible on the
assumption that the division of letters into separate words
was not always strictly adhered to in some early manuscripts.
It is reasonable to hold that, had there been a clear division
of words, this double haplography would not have occurred.
Turning now to the text in Psalm 18, we have to find some
rational explanation for the interpolation of the word לְפָנָיו
'before him'. This looks like a note telling the reader that the

expression 'shall come into his [God's] ears' means 'shall come before him'. One has the impression that this note was originally written in above the words תָּבֹא בְאָזְנָיו and was later copied in by a copyist. The religious authorities responsible for this note must have known that the word בְּאָזְנָיו in this context means 'in his hearing' since, in Hebrew, many abstract ideas are expressed in concrete terms. Yet, because they feared that the reader might take this phrase literally and think of God in anthromorphic terms, they took the precaution of providing this explanatory note. It would seem that this precaution was especially necessary when Hebrew had ceased to be a living language, confined to the spheres of prayer and the reading of the Scriptures, and the reader might understand the words literally. Because this word causes a break in the smooth flow of the poet's thought, we pronounce it to be a gloss. The *LXX* version represents both the defective reading of the 2 Samuel text and the incorporated gloss of the Psalms text (enumerated as 17). The JB translation in both texts, the RSV in the Samuel text 'my cry came to his ears', and the NEB 'my cry reached his ears' in the Psalms text are in accordance with the above restoration.

Another example of this kind of gloss is found in Amos 6: 8, where we read נִשְׁבַּע אֲדֹנָי יֱהֹוִה בְּנַפְשׁוֹ נְאֻם יהוה צְבָאוֹת 'The Lord God had sworn by himself [or by his life], *says the Lord, God of hosts*, I loathe the arrogance of Jacob'. The second Hebrew expression, represented by the translation in italics, is to be regarded as a gloss. One would say that the intent of this explanatory note was to remove any trace of an anthropomorphism from the expression in the first part of the verse. The fact that it is not represented in the *LXX* version tends to confirm this conclusion, apart from its disturbing the free flow of thought and overburdening the verse. The NEB omits this phrase and the RSV places it in brackets, both versions regarding it as a gloss. That this gloss is not a variant reading may be inferred from the general usage of this formula at the *end* of an oracle and not as an introduction to it.

The epithet אֲדֹנָי יֱהֹוִה is found also in the massoretic text of Isaiah 3: 15 at the end of the verse (and elsewhere) and is explained by the corresponding wording in the Qumran text of Isaiah. In the latter we find it as יהוה֞ אֲדוֹנָי , a clear directive to the reader to read the divine name יהוה 'YHWH' as אדוני 'Lord'; obviously, the word written above the line was never meant to be part of the text. However, as we see from the massoretic text, the copyist wrote in both words, so that the second word had now to be read as אֱלֹהִים 'God'. Following the usual practice in pointed Hebrew of supplying the consonants of the $k^e t\hat{\imath}b$ in the text with the vowel-points of the $k^e r\hat{e}$ which was to be read, the impossible word יֱהֹוִה was produced. The reader was thus expected to read this word as directed.

(*b*) Our next example of glosses indicate that some variant traditional readings of the authorized text, though not accepted as official readings, were nevertheless considered worthy of note. The Massoretes of a later age followed this practice by providing in their textual notes a number of variant readings which were thought to be of some value and merited their being mentioned. Our first example is in 1 Samuel 12. Following upon the election of Saul as the first king of Israel by Samuel, in response to the demand by the elders that he should appoint a king over the people to lead them in battle against the formidable Philistines, the prophet delivers a sermon reproaching them for their insistent request. In verse 12 he states 'You said "no, but a king shall rule over us" [see 8: 19b], though the Lord, your God is your king.' Continuing in verse 13, according to the massoretic Hebrew text, he says: 'and now here is your king whom you have chosen, whom you requested [or demanded]'— אֲשֶׁר בְּחַרְתֶּם אֲשֶׁר שְׁאֶלְתֶּם . One immediately observes that one of these two phrases would have been adequate. This observation, coupled with the fact that the *LXX* rendered only the first phrase, points to two variant traditional readings with different implications. The one suggests that the choice of Saul as the first king of Israel was made by the people and not by divine guidance through the mediation of Samuel. The other version implies that only the request for a king was made by the people, but that the choice of the man to fill this high office was not made by them but by God. The *LXX* rendering indicates that in the text before the translators the original wording was 'whom you have chosen'. We conclude then that, if this was the original massoretic phrase, the other reading 'whom you demanded' was known and considered worthy of preservation. It was written above the accepted reading as an exegetical note, reminding the reader that the choice of Saul by the people was the result of their demand for a king. The reverse is, of course, possible, namely that the reading rendered by the *LXX* was the alternative one. It follows, then, that some copyist wrote in this note alongside the original reading. We thus have a gloss which we would place in the category of variant traditional readings. The JB follows the *LXX* in retaining only the first reading. Occasionally a variant reading incorporated into a text may be indicated by the agreement between the two readings in part and their differing in part, as here. There is the possibility, however, that the second phrase is an interpretative note on the first, influenced by the statement in 8: 5 that the selection of a king by Samuel was requested by the leaders of the people.

A similar incident of a variant reading having been incorporated into a text occurred in the Qumran text of Isaiah, chapter 14, verse 2. The massoretic text reads וּלְקָחוּם עַמִּים וֶהֱבִיאוּם אֶל־מְקוֹמָם 'and nations shall take them and bring them to their place [JB, to the place they came from]. The Targum rendering (וְיוֹבְלוּנוּן) לְאַרְעֲהוֹן '[and they shall bring them] to their land' presupposes a Hebrew reading of either לְאַרְצָם or לְאַדְמָתָם. The Qumran text reads ולקחום עמים רבים והביאום אל אדמתם ואל מקומם 'and *many* nations shall take them and bring them *to their land and to their place'*. Apart from the exaggeration introduced by the additional word רַבִּים 'many', the Qumran text displays the readings of both the massoretic text and the one which seems to have underlaid the Targum. We suggest that, originally, there was only one authorized read-ing in this text, but the authorities at Qumran were aware of the other traditional reading which they regarded as worthy of preserving. The alternative reading must have been written in as a textual note above the accepted reading and was some time later incorporated into the text by a copyist.

(*c*) We now come to the third type of gloss—that is, a note meant to extend or develop the thought of the writer and influenced by pious sentiments. This type of gloss is well illustrated in the Song of Hannah in 1 Samuel 2: 2, where we find the poetic verse אֵין קָדוֹשׁ כַּיהוה כִּי אֵין בִּלְתֶּךָ וְאֵין צוּר כֵּאלֹהֵינוּ 'there is none holy like the Lord, *for there is none beside thee, and there is no rock* [? or creator[1]] like our God'. In examining this verse one would say that the first and third parts balance each other in accordance with the rules of parallelism in ancient Hebrew poetry and that the intervening line breaks this paral-lelism. Our pronouncing this line to be a gloss is reinforced by its presence in the *LXX* version, not in the middle of the verse, however, but at the end of it. The difference of the location of this line may be explained by its having originally been a note written above the verse and, while a copyist of the text which became the massoretic incorporated it between the two halves of the verse, the copyist of the text which became the one used by the *LXX* translators copied it in at the end of the verse. The note itself may be described as a pious credal statement to reinforce the words of the poet. Sometimes interpolated notes in the Hebrew text are recog-nized by introductory words, such as כִּי 'for', 'because', לָכֵן or עַל־כֵּן 'therefore', and לְמַעַן 'in order that'.

We take this discussion a stage further by referring to the discovery in the fourth cave at Qumran of a fragmentary Hebrew text of 1 Samuel in only two columns, including the

---

[1] The talmudic tractate Berakot 10a notes, on this verse, that צוּר means צַיָּר "fashioner" from the root יָצַר–and so 'creator'.

verse under examination here.[2] We note firstly that, in the
LXX version of chapter 2, verse 2, the Greek reading δίκαιος
'righteous' represents the Hebrew word צַדִּיק and not the
massoretic צוּר. That is to say, it had the word צדק (without
the vowel-letter) in its Hebrew text, whereas the massoretic
text had צר –a confusion at least between ד and ר. It may be
that this presents a better balance with the adjective קָדוֹשׁ 'holy'
in the first half of the verse. However, what is rather surprising
is that the Qumran fragment has both readings, namely
אֵין צַדִּיק כֵּאלֹהֵינוּ of the *LXX* rendering and וְאֵין צוּר כֵּאלֹהֵינוּ of
the massoretic text. The explanation of this conflated Qum-
ran text may be as follows. The original reading of the Qumran
fragment was the one underlying the *LXX* rendering, but the
authorities knew of the reading which became the one in the
massoretic tradition and this variant was written in above the
line as a textual note of interest. A copyist of the Qumran
text of Samuel, however, copied it along with the established
reading. We would say, then, that this Qumran fragment of 1
Samuel provides us with a dual gloss. The one is a pious note
and the other a reference to a variant reading of some worth.
As suggested earler (p. 84) the disagreement between the
two expressions in only one word indicates variant readings.

In Psalm 51: 16 the text reads 'Deliver me from bloodshed,
O God, *my God of salvation*—אֱלֹהֵי תְּשׁוּעָתִי—and my tongue
shall sing your praises'. The two Hebrew words, translated in
italics, are an intrusion into the text and upset the balance of
the two halves. If we ignore them the two halves of the verse
complement each other admirably. This note, which was at
some time incorporated into the text by a copyist, is a pious
sentiment, extending the thought of the poet. It states that
God, to whom the poet directs his prayer, is a 'God of salvation', so that his plea for deliverance will be answered in a
divine act of salvation.

[2] Frank Cross in *Bulletin of the American Schools of Oriental Research* no. 132,
December, 1953, pp. 15ff.

Extra Note. The following gloss has not been placed in any
defined category, for it is the only example of its kind that
we have found. It may be that other examples may come to
light but for the time being we have to treat it as a special
kind of gloss. We describe it as a proto-massoretic note
which had become embodied in the text. Our reference is
Psalm 61: 8 which reads in the first half of the verse, with
reference to the king, 'May he abide for ever in the presence
of the Lord'. The second half of the verse, in the massoretic
Hebrew text, is חֶסֶד וֶאֱמֶת מַן יִנְצְרֻהוּ. The word מַן poses a serious
difficulty. As it stands it is the shortened Imperative Piel
form of the verb מָנָה with the general meaning 'appoint'. Consequently the RSV translates this line as '*bid* steadfast love
and faithfulness watch over him', while the JB renders it 'assign
your love and faithfulness to guard Him'. The *LXX* translators
were baffled by this Hebrew word which, in fact, they took
to be the normal Aramaic word for 'who?'. The problem is
resolved very simply when we realize that we have not a
Hebrew word in this text but a mnemonic מ״ן standing for
מָלֵא נוּן 'Nun Plene'. This note points out that whereas normally the vowelless נ is assimilated (and the following letter
generally doubled), in this special case the letter is *un*assimilated and the traditional form of this word in this text is יִנְצְרֻהוּ
instead of the expected יִצְּרֻהוּ.[3] This prayer or hope for the
king's well-being was expressed in the same formula found in
Proverbs 20: 28 as חֶסֶד וֶאֱמֶת יִצְּרוּ מֶלֶךְ 'Loyalty and faithfulness guard the king.' We would thus describe the word מן as a
proto-massoretic note written above the word referred to and
was copied into the text by a copyist. Once again it is to be
noted that, since this gloss was in the Hebrew text before the
LXX translators, it was well established in the text at that
time and is therefore much older. It is of interest that this
gloss points to a kind of massoretic activity going back at least

[3] Cf. Julius Fuerst, *A Hebrew and Chaldaic Lexicon to the Old Testament,* 4th
edition, translated from the German by Samuel Davidson (London: Williams &
Norgate, 1871), p. 831.

to the third or second centuries BC. The NEB translation ignores this word, thereby indicating the recognition of its being a gloss.

(*d*) We now turn to an examination of editorial notes. The first observation to be made is that though such notes are mainly of the same character as glosses they do not constitute breaks in the writer's thoughts but are generally addenda to them. They were seemingly attached to verses as editorial policy. Our first example of an editorial note is found in Psalm 1 at the end of verse 3. The poet describes as follows the fortunes of the pious man who shuns the company of sinners but whose delight is in God's Tora: 'He shall be like a tree planted over streams of water, whose fruit it gives forth in its season and whose leaf does not wither'. Then comes what appears to be an addendum וְכֹל אֲשֶׁר יַעֲשֶׂה יַצְלִיחַ 'whatever he does he will be successful'. We note that this last clause is in prose, in contrast to the rest of the verse which is poetry. It may be explained as orginally a note designed to point out that, in practical terms, what the poet meant to convey in his description of the pious man as an evergreen flourishing tree was that whatever he undertook he would be successful. This final clause does not break the continuity of the thought in the verses; it is an addendum to it and is to be described as an explanatory editorial note deliberately attached to the verse.

The presence of an editorial note in the massoretic Hebrew text of Isaiah 2: 9 is very likely to be detected in the light of the Qumran recension of this book. The verse reads '[mortal] man shall be humbled and [superior] man shall be brought low'. The massoretic text has the addition וְאַל תִּשָּׂא לָהֶם 'but do not forgive them'. These words are not in the Qumran version. Considering the many instances of omissions in the Qumran text through carelessness, it might be thought that here we have another example of a copyist's omission. Yet the fact that these words were not supplied by a later hand— as were recognized omissions in the Qumran text of Isaiah— indicates that they did not exist in their recension. It looks very much as if we have here an editorial note appended to the verse in the massoretic text with the intent of reinforcing the severity of the fate to be suffered by idolaters, in that God will not relent but will withold forgiveness from them. The *LXX* rendered this clause as 'but *I* will not pardon them', thereby reading אֶשָּׂא for תִשָּׂא.

Glosses and editorial notes are not confined to the Hebrew text of the Bible, but are found also in the *LXX* version. They proliferate in particular in the *LXX* version of the book of Proverbs. A few examples in English translation will suffice to illustrate this remarkable feature. Proverbs 1: 7 reads 'The fear of the Lord is the beginning of knowledge; but fools scorn wisdom and discipline'. The *LXX* rendering of this verse is quite correct but it is preceded by a quotation from Psalm 111: 10, namely 'The fear of the Lord is the beginning of wisdom; those who practise it have sound sense.' In 3: 9 we read 'Honour the Lord with your wealth and with the first fruits of your produce.' The *LXX* has 'Honour the Lord with your *just* labours; give him the first of your fruits of *righteousness.*' The italicized words are explanatory notes of a pious nature incorporated into the text. In 10: 10 the massoretic text states that 'he who winks with his eyes causes trouble.' The *LXX* rendering 'he who winks with his eyes *deceitfully . . .*'. The additional word represented by the italicized translation is, clearly, an explanatory note copied into the body of the text. There are many more instances of addenda in the *LXX* version of Proverbs and this phenomenon points to the same kind of proto-rabbinic literary activity in the *LXX* that we find in the massoretic Hebrew Bible.

7

THE PHILOLOGICAL APPROACH

REFERENCE was made earlier to the impact of philological studies on textual problems. It was pointed out that when confronted with a strange word or with a familiar word in a Hebrew text which produces either nonsense or an unacceptable meaning, the scholar will look to other Semitic languages to ascertain whether the enigmatic word was in the vocabulary of a sister language with a meaning which fits the context in the biblical text under study. To illustrate this approach we cite the verb יָדַע 'knew' which does not suit the context of Judges 16: 9. In this chapter Delilah presses Samson to reveal to her the secret of his prodigious strength, with the aim of betraying him to the Philistines. He tells her that if he were bound by fresh bow-strings which had not yet been dried, he would lose his strength and become like an ordinary man (v. 7). This she did, but he snapped them asunder easily and, then, the narrator says וְלֹא נוֹדַע כֹּחוֹ (v. 9) which, taken literally, means 'his strength was not known'. To give these words the meaning required by the context the RSV and the JB take them to mean *the secret of* his strength was not known'. However, scholars have pointed to a verb in Arabic—*waduᶜa*—meaning 'was low, humbled' which, it is suggested, had existed in the Hebrew vocabulary but, because of its close similarity with the familiar verb הידע-דע was wrongly identified with it when Hebrew was no longer a spoken language, and was consequently lost. They point out that it is most likely this verb *waduᶜa* which the narrator used in the Samson story and the Niphal (passive) form of this verb would yield the sense that 'his strength was not brought low'. This understanding of the line suits the context admirably. Delilah had expected Samson to become weakened but his strength was unimpaired.

Another text where the verb *waduᶜa* is appropriate to the

theme of the verse rather than the verb ידע is Isaiah 53: 3. The
plight of the Suffering Servant is described as 'despised and
rejected by men, a man of sorrows [or pain] and וִידוּעַ חֹלִי
which the RSV translates 'acquainted with grief' and the JB
'familiar with suffering'. The difficulty with both renderings
is that the form ידוע is a passive participle and means 'known',
referring to the suffering and not to the experience of the
sufferer. When, however, we take this verb to be the redis-
covered *waduᶜa* 'was low', the passive participle suits the context well, for it means 'brought low, humbled by sickness'.

Yet, a philologically suggested solution to a textual difficulty may sometimes pose an unexpected problem to the
scholar. To illustrate a case in point we turn to Judges 8: 16.
In the earlier part of the chapter we learn of the pursuit of
the two fugitive kings of Midian by the charismatic leader
Gideon. He and his men pause at the town of Sukkoth, from
whose authorities he requested food for his weary men. This
request was met by a haughty rebuff by the notables of the
town. Gideon, enraged at their refusal and their insolent
attitude, made the following threat. When the two kings are
captured 'I will thresh (וְדַשְׁתִּי), [i.e. flail] your bodies with
desert thorns and briers' (v. 7). Having caught the two fugitive
kings, Gideon returned to Sukkoth to carry out his threatened
punishment. The text then describes in v. 16 how he took
desert thorns and briers and, in the Hebrew וַיֹּדַע בָּהֶם אֵת־אַנְשֵׁי
סֻכּוֹת . If this is the familiar verb יָדַע the sense of this line would
be 'he caused the men of Sukkoth to know' which is modified
by the RSV to 'he taught the men of Sukkoth'. One would
have to interpret the sense to mean something like 'he taught
them a lesson', as we would say. This is stretching the sense
of this causative (Hiphil) form of ידע 'knew' too far. When
one turns to the ancient versions one finds that the *LXX* rendered this word ἠλόησεν 'he tore or bruised the men of Sukkoth', while the Targum has תַּבַּר 'he broke the men of Sukkoth'.
In another context (Psalm 43: 3) we have the word תָּרַע 'Thou
dost break', which the Targum renders תַּבַּרְתָּ 'thou hast broken'.

It is therefore likely that in our reference the Targum read וַיָּרַע 'and he broke', reading a ר for a ד. The *LXX* version seems to suggest a Hebrew reading וַיָּדָשׁ 'and he threshed' which is in keeping with the narrative. Gideon threatened to thresh (or flail) them with desert thorns and briers and this is precisely what we would have expected him to do when he returned to Sukkoth to carry out his threat. The emendation from וידע to וידש in the consonantal text is slight, affecting only the last letter of the word and, therefore, does not do much violence to the word. Apparently supported by the *LXX*, it was accepted by the JB which translated 'and he tore the men of Sukkoth with them'.

Yet, the problem is by no means solved to the satisfaction of all scholars, for there are some who hold that here, too, we have the verb *wadu^c a* 'was low, humble' in the Hiphîl (causative)—that is, 'he humiliated the men of Sukkoth'. On this understanding of the verb Gideon's revenge was that he humiliated these notables in response to the arrogance they displayed towards him when he needed their help.

It should be stressed that the textual critic welcomes a philological solution to a given textual difficulty, for this leaves the text intact. It is only when a copyist's error is clearly obvious that he feels entitled to make the necessary adjustment or, when he is satisfied that a corruption had somehow been introduced into the text and he cannot account for it that he reluctantly, and tentatively, offers a conjectural emendation which would be based on careful consideration. In our text in Judges 8: 16 he has to make his choice between two competing solutions. On the one hand, the proposed emendation is what one might have expected the writer to say and it looks as if the *LXX* supports it, while, on the other hand, the philological solution leaves the text intact and also adds a new dimension to the vengence wreaked on the Sukkoth notables by Gideon. There is also to be taken into account the possibility that in the Hebrew text before translators of the *LXX* version the word was וידע, but that they adapted their translations to suit the context as they understood it. It is not to be taken for granted that translators of the ancient versions always translated the Hebrew before them literally, for they not infrequently had recourse to interpretation when faced with a difficult reading. It is not beyond the bounds of possibility that the translators faced the same problem as modern critics did before philology was brought into play by the latter and that they felt impelled to interpret this awkward word in terms of the narrative in verse 9 to bring it into harmony with it and that, in doing so, they believed they were presenting the intent of the writer.

Examples of the application of the philological approach could be multiplied. Learned journals teem with samples of biblical texts which had been condemned as corrupt but which were subsequently found to be correct in the light of new knowledge emanating from the comparative study of Semitic languages. That is to say, lost meanings were restored. Yet one must not assume that philology holds the key to every textual difficulty. Though some of the alleged restored meanings of Hebrew words may be the result of ingenious comparison with parallel words in other Semitic languages, caution and restraint must be exercised by the scholar. The student who wishes to have a variety of samples of solutions offered by the philological method should read Professor James Barr's excellent book on *Comparative Philology and the Text of the Old Testament* (see bibliography).

Earlier two examples were given of the recovered meaning of the verb יָדַע. For a comprehensive discussion of the impact of philology on textual problems connected with this verb as it appears in several biblical texts, the student should study the article by Professor J.A. Emerton entitled 'A Consideration of some alleged meanings of the verb יָדַע in Hebrew' in the *Journal of Semitic Studies*, volume XV, no. 2. Much of the article deals with the researches of the later Professor D. Winton Thomas and others on the meaning of this verb in contexts where the usual sense 'to know' is inappropriate and where the context itself is not helpful in determining its derived meaning.

CONCLUDING REMARKS

IN the examination of any human situation where irregularities are brought to light, there is always the danger of the impression being created that the irregularities are dominant features in the character of the subject examined and some doubt might be cast on his quality and reliability. It should therefore be stated explicitly that, when we survey the Hebrew Bible as a whole, the incidence of copyists' errors is statistically very few indeed. Even allowing for the intrusion of occasional errors in the received Hebrew text, it is remarkable how faithfully it was transmitted. It should also be borne in mind that the textual critic, when faced with a difficult text, will in the first place try to make sense of it as it stands. If, within the range of his knowledge, he finds this impossible, he will only then have recourse to the apparatus of Textual Criticism. When philology fails to resolve the particular textual difficulty, he will turn to the appropriate avenue of investigation in his endeavour to restore the correct text.

In much of the foregoing chapters we have dealt with identifiable types of copyists' errors in the text of the massoretic Hebrew Bible and we have offered appropriate corrections in accordance with the guide-lines laid down. The cases dealt with are selected samples of the kind of miscopying which the student will come across in the course of his critical studies of the Hebrew text. It is hoped that he will recognize these types of error and will see how the apparatus appropriate to the situation is applied and the necessary correction thereby achieved.

Clearly it has not been possible to deal with all known types of error in the biblical text in a book designed as an Introduction to the Science of Textual Criticism. The aim of this book is to provide a general understanding of what Textual Criticism is concerned with and to deal with types of error most common in the text of the Hebrew Bible. Perhaps the most unsatisfactory element in this area of textual studies is conjectural emendation. In many instances the student finds himself confronted with a variety of emendations differing from each other and each claiming some validity. Unless there are convincing reasons for the preference of one emendation against the others, one should perhaps note all of them and suspend judgement in the confident expectation that, one day, the right solution will be found.

98

BIBLIOGRAPHY

BARR, JAMES, *Comparative Philology and the Text of the Old Testament*, Clarendon Press, Oxford, 1968.

CROSS, FRANK M., 'A new Qumran biblical fragment related to the original Hebrew underlying the Septuagint', *Bulletin of the American Schools of Oriental Research*, 132 (December 1953).

EMERTON, J.A., 'A Consideration of some alleged meanings of the verb יָדַע in Hebrew', *Journal of Semitic Studies*, XV.2 (1970).

FUERST, JULIUS, *A Hebrew and Chaldaic Lexicon of the Old Testament*, 4th edition, translated from the German by Samuel Davidson, Williams and Norgate, London, 1871.

KENNICOTT, B., *Collation of Hebrew Manuscripts of the Old Testament, 1761-69*, Oxford, 1770.

ROBERTS, B.J., *The Old Testament Text and Versions*, University of Wales Press, Cardiff, 1951.

ROSSI DE J.B., *Apparatus Hebraeo-Biblicus*, Parma 1782.

THOMAS, WINTON D., 'The textual criticism of the Old Testament', *The Old Testament and Modern Study*, Clarendon Press, Oxford, 1951.

THOMPSON, J.A., 'Textual criticism in the Old Testament', *The Interpreters' Dictionary of the Bible*, Supplementary volume, Abingdon, Nashville, U.S.A., 1976.

WEINGREEN, J., 'Interpretation, history of, within the Old Testament', *The Interpreters' Dictionary of the Bible*, Supplementary volume, Abingdon, Nashville, U.S.A., 1976.

– *From Bible to Mishna – the Continuity of Tradition*, Manchester University Press, 1976.

INDEX OF SUBJECTS

INDEX OF REFERENCES